PREPARATION FOR THE
END TIME

Some other books by Norman R. Gulley

Christ Is Coming! A Christ-Centered Approach to Last-Day Events

Christ Our Refuge: Making It Safely Through the Last Days

Christ, Our Substitute

Final Events on Planet Earth

Satan's Trojan Horse: God's End-Time Victory

Systematic Theology: The Church and the Last Things, vol. 4

PREPARATION FOR THE
END TIME

NORMAN R. GULLEY

Cover design resources from Lars Justinen

Unless otherwise indicated, all Scripture quotations are from THE HOLY BIBLE, NEW INTERNATIONAL VERSION®. Copyright © 1973, 1978, 1984, 2011 by Biblica, Inc®. Used by permission. All rights reserved worldwide.

Scripture quotations marked ESV are from The Holy Bible, English Standard Version®. ESV® Permanent Text Edition® (2016). Copyright © 2001 by Crossway Bibles, a publishing ministry of Good News Publishers.

Scripture quotations marked KJV are from the King James Version of the Bible.

Scripture quotations marked NKJV are from the New King James Version®. Copyright © 1982 by Thomas Nelson. Used by permission. All rights reserved.

Scripture quotations marked RSV are from the Revised Standard Version of the Bible, copyright © 1946, 1952, 1971 by the Division of Christian Education of the National Council of the Churches of Christ in the U.S.A. Used by permission.

Additional copies of this book are available by calling toll-free 1-800-765-6955 or by visiting http://www.AdventistBookCenter.com.

ISBN 978-0-8163-6106-9

October 2017

Dedication

Dedicated to my wonderful wife,

precious four children,

nine grandchildren, and two greats,

and to all who love Christ deeply and long for His soon coming.

Contents

Preface

May God abundantly bless us as we prepare for the Second Advent. Endless joy, peace, and security are just ahead! We'll be with the Father, Son, and Holy Spirit as well as our loved ones, friends, angels, inhabitants of unnumbered worlds, and the redeemed. Let's not miss it!

CHAPTER 1

The Cosmic Controversy

When I was just a little lad in England, I was gazing at the sky from my bedroom window and asked my mother, "What is eternity? And how long is it?"

"It's forever," Mother replied with a smile.

"How could it be?" I puzzled. "Everything has a beginning and an end. Eternity is impossible!"

That night I dreamed I entered heaven and joined others on a nonstop beltway called eternity. Once on the belt I couldn't get off. Fear gripped me. Feeling trapped, I yelled, "Let me off!" That cry woke me up and *whew*, what relief! But I was still puzzled.

Is Christ eternal? When Proverbs 8:22 mentions that "the Lord brought me forth as the first of his works," does this mean that the heavenly Father brought forth His Son in past eternity? If so, Christ had a beginning.

Writing in a magazine article, Ellen G. White referred to Christ's words "I AM" as signifying an eternal self-existence. She said, "Christ is the pre-existent, self-existent Son of God." She continued, "In speaking of His pre-existence, Christ carries the mind back through dateless ages. He assures us that there never was a time when He was not in close fellowship with the eternal God."[1] Six years later she reiterated that Christ

11

"existed from eternity, a distinct person."[2]

Hence, Christ wasn't brought forth from the Father. Rather, Christ's life is "original, unborrowed, underived."[3] That agrees with the Bible: Christ is "from everlasting" (Micah 5:2, KJV), and He is also called the "Everlasting Father" (Isaiah 9:6).

Lucifer's rebellion

The cosmic controversy began in the heart of Lucifer (he is also called *Satan*, which means "the adversary"). As a mere created being, he wanted to replace the eternal Christ. But Christ had an endless eternity of experience as God; Christ had a "glorious high throne from the beginning" (Jeremiah 17:12, KJV). Satan had nothing of the kind.

Christ also "created and upheld the unnumbered worlds through the vast realms of space."[4] How could Lucifer rule the universe when he can't even create a blade of grass and when he isn't omnipresent? He's confined to one place and thus totally unqualified! He wanted to replace his Creator, who created all things (Colossians 1:16; Hebrews 1:2). What audacity Satan had!

In spite of these issues, "little by little Lucifer came to indulge the desire for self-exaltation."[5] "You [Lucifer] have said in your heart, . . . 'I will exalt my throne above the stars of God; . . . I will be like the Most High'" (Isaiah 14:13, 14, NKJV). Lucifer "ventured to covet homage due alone to the Creator."[6]

Blind pride goaded Satan's hatred of Christ. "He was a murderer from the beginning" (John 8:44). What does this mean? If possible, he would have killed Christ in heaven. "To dispute the supremacy of the Son of God, thus impeaching the wisdom and love of the Creator, had become the purpose of this prince of angels."[7] He charged God as "severe and tyrannical."[8] He denounced God's law "as a restriction of their liberty and declared that it was his purpose to secure the abolition of law." Thus, "the hosts of heaven might enter upon a more exalted, more glorious state of existence."[9]

Just look at Satan's grandiose plans: "God's government

included not only the inhabitants of heaven, but of all the worlds that He had created; and Lucifer had concluded that if he could carry the angels of heaven with him in rebellion, he also could carry all the worlds."[10]

In response, the King of the universe called all the angels together to explain that Christ was equally divine as Himself and that They had created all the worlds together. In this work, Christ had not sought exaltation for Himself.[11]

> The angels joyfully acknowledged the supremacy of Christ. . . . Lucifer bowed with them, but in his heart there was a strange, fierce conflict. . . . The influence of the holy angels seemed for a time to carry him with them. As songs of praise ascended in melodious strains, swelled by thousands of glad voices, the spirit of evil seemed vanquished; unutterable love thrilled his entire being; his soul went out, in harmony with the sinless worshippers, in love to the Father and the Son. But again he was filled with pride in his own glory. His desire for supremacy returned, and envy of Christ was once more indulged.[12]

Christ loved Lucifer with infinite love and "yearning pity."[13] He longed to save him. "Long was he [Satan] retained in heaven. Again and again he was offered pardon on condition of repentance and submission."[14] "Lucifer was convinced that he was in the wrong. . . . He nearly reached the decision to return, but pride forbade him."[15] Finally, he was forced to leave.

After his dismissal from heaven, Lucifer asked for an interview with Christ, and it was granted. He wanted to be reinstated in heaven, and Christ wept at his condition. No doubt his claim in heaven to provide a higher existence of liberty was not what he experienced. He had lost the joy sinless beings had in being united with Christ. Also his rebellion had reached an incurable state.[16] Christ loved His enemy. He shed tears for him, but Lucifer responded with hate.

It was these two sides of the controversy—love and

hate—that needed to be fully revealed to all created beings in the vast universe. Satan's rebellion in heaven had been under the guise of loyalty.[17] He needed to be fully unmasked. At the same time, the charges made against Christ needed to be shown as false.

This is why Satan was allowed to live on and not receive the wages of death for his treacherous sin against Christ. If Satan had received those wages, created beings would have wondered whether the claims that God is tyrannical and severe were true. There would be no resolution to the cosmic controversy. Full exposure and full revelation of the two sides of the controversy were the only way to resolve the strife. "For the good of the entire universe through ceaseless ages Satan must more fully develop his principles, that his charges against the divine government might be seen in their true light by all created beings, that the justice and mercy of God and the immutability of His law might forever be placed beyond all question."[18]

In heaven, Lucifer's campaign against Christ was based on change. He claimed he could provide a better future under his leadership than that offered by Christ. Change was the offer made to the angels, and many were deceived by Lucifer. But it was a false promise:

> "God is love." 1 John 4:16. His nature, His law, is love. It ever has been; it ever will be. "The high and lofty One that inhabiteth eternity," whose "ways are everlasting," changeth not. With Him "is no variableness, neither shadow of turning." Isaiah 57:15; Habakkuk 3:6; James 1:17. . . .
>
> The history of the great conflict between good and evil, from the time it first began in heaven to the final overthrow of rebellion and the total eradication of sin, is also a demonstration of God's unchanging love.[19]

God's unchanging love exposes Lucifer's false campaign. "God desires from all His creatures the service of love—service

14

that springs from an appreciation of His character. He takes no pleasure in a forced obedience; and to all He grants freedom of will, that they may render Him voluntary service."[20] What patience, what wisdom, what love God has!

Seduction in a garden

Think of the differing statements that Christ and Satan made in Eden. Christ said, "Eat, and you will die!" (see Genesis 2:16, 17). Satan blatantly disagreed: "Eat, and you will not die!" (see Genesis 3:4, 5). Lucifer began the cosmic controversy on planet Earth by questioning God's word and has continued the practice throughout human history.

Unlike Satan, Christ loved Adam and Eve. To protect them from Satan's scheming, Christ sent two angels to warn them about Satan and to tell them "that they could obey the law of God and be inexpressibly happy, or disobey and lose their high estate and be plunged into hopeless despair."[21]

Adam and Eve said they would never disobey God's command, "for it was their highest pleasure to do His will."[22] God promised that "if necessary, every angel from heaven would come to their help rather than that he [Satan] should in any way do them harm."[23]

But Satan was crafty. In those days, serpents flew through the air and had a dazzling appearance. Satan took the form of a beautiful serpent in order to deceive Adam and Eve. While in the shape of a serpent, he "took his position in the tree of knowledge and commenced leisurely eating of the fruit."[24]

What a setup Satan created! He was eating the forbidden fruit. But Christ had said to Adam, "You are free to eat from any tree in the garden; but you must not eat from the tree of the knowledge of good and evil, for when you eat from it you will certainly die" (Genesis 2:16, 17). And "the angels [had] cautioned Eve not to separate from her husband."[25] Yet when she realized she had separated herself from him, "she thought herself secure, even if she did not remain close by the side of her husband. She had wisdom and strength to know if evil came, and to meet it."[26] She had not only moved away from

Adam's side but also from Christ's presence. She was in grave danger. Her self-dependence was already disobedience, even prior to transgressing Christ's warning that she would die if she ate the fruit from the forbidden tree.

Eve came to the forbidden tree, gazed at the fruit with "curiosity and admiration," and wondered "why God had so decidedly prohibited their eating and touching it."[27] After all, the serpent was eating the fruit and was very much alive. The serpent also claimed it was able to speak because it ate the fruit.[28]

Note Satan's trap: Eve believed what she saw more than what she had been told. Seeing is believing! Eve considered the serpent speaking human language and not dying from eating the fruit to be compelling empirical evidence. The serpent also "extolled her beauty and exceeding loveliness, which was not displeasing to Eve."[29] What flattery Satan employs!

Eve listened. She must have thought, *If a serpent can speak my human language through eating the fruit, think of what I will become—I will become as God* (see Genesis 3:5). Heady stuff, indeed! It seemed that God was keeping her back from her full potential. In other words, the snake appeared to be more interested in helping her than was Christ, her Creator.

By this point, Eve's mind had been invaded by deception. Thus, "Eve was not horror-stricken to hear the holy and supreme God thus falsely accused. If she had turned her thoughts toward God . . . and remembered all the tokens of his love, . . . she might have been saved. . . . One word in vindication of her Creator would have caused the accuser to flee."[30] Instead, Eve "saw that the fruit of the tree was good for food and pleasing to the eye, and also desirable for gaining wisdom, she took some and ate it" (Genesis 3:6).

Eve believed in a stranger who had given her nothing and disbelieved her Creator who had given her everything. "Eve was beguiled, flattered, infatuated."[31] That's the power of "seeing is believing." Eve should have remembered Christ's words, "Eat, and you will die." Believing Christ's words would have given her discernment to distrust the deception. For believing God's Word would have helped her to see through the counterfeit.

Battleground in the human mind

The cosmic controversy on planet Earth takes place in the mind, just as it did in heaven. The fact that the angels and Adam and Eve were victims of this battle proves that deception can have a powerful influence on perfect minds. How much more powerful deception must be on imperfect, fallen minds!

As previously noted, "seeing is believing" is a powerful tool among Satan's methods of deception because what we look at makes an impression on our minds. Impure television shows, films, and novels can corrupt our minds and thus feed our fallen nature. We must choose wisely, for feeding the mind with poison is just as damaging as feeding poison to the body. We reap what we sow (see Galatians 6:7).

Yet we have reason for hope! Our ticket for heaven was paid by Christ at Calvary. It was the highest price that Christ could pay. No one else could pay such a price. It is available for us, and it is free. When we choose Jesus, His power becomes ours. The clever deceiver is no match for a heart protected by the Son of God. Jesus provides the power to choose wisely and foil the temptations of Satan. In a fallen world, Satan gives us failure and guilt, whereas Christ gives us His powerful presence to receive freedom and salvation.

> The Elder Brother [Christ] of our race is by the eternal throne. He looks upon every soul who is turning his face toward Him as the Saviour. He knows by experience what are the weaknesses of humanity, what are our wants, and where lies the strength of our temptations; for He was in all points tempted like as we are, yet without sin. He is watching over you, trembling child of God. Are you tempted? He will deliver. Are you weak? He will strengthen. Are you ignorant? He will enlighten. Are you wounded? He will heal. . . .
>
>   . . . Our heavenly Father has a thousand ways to provide for us, of which we know nothing. Those who

accept the one principle of making the service and honor of God supreme will find perplexities vanish, and a plain path before their feet.[32]

Paul pointed to the ultimate focus for our minds: "We all, with unveiled face, beholding the glory of the Lord, are being transformed into the same image from one degree of glory to another. For this comes from the Lord who is the Spirit" (2 Corinthians 3:18, ESV). By continuing to behold Christ, we are continually being changed to be like Him, so that "when he appears we shall be like him" (1 John 3:2, ESV).

The cosmic controversy rages on and neutrality is not an option. Every human must make their choice, a choice that centers on accepting Jesus Christ as a personal savior. Now is the perfect time to strengthen your heart and mind with God's Word. "None but those who have fortified the mind with the truths of the Bible will stand through the last great conflict."[33]

1. Ellen G. White, "Resistance to Light, No. 3," *Signs of the Times*, August 29, 1900, 2, 3.

2. Ellen G. White, "The Word Made Flesh," *Review and Herald*, April 5, 1906, 8.

3. Ellen G. White, *The Desire of Ages* (Mountain View, CA: Pacific Press® Pub. Assn., 1898), 530.

4. Ellen G. White, *The Great Controversy* (Mountain View, CA: Pacific Press® Pub. Assn., 1911), 651.

5. Ellen G. White, *Patriarchs and Prophets* (Mountain View, CA: Pacific Press® Pub. Assn., 1890), 35. See also Ezekiel 28:17.

6. White, *Patriarchs and Prophets*, 35.

7. Ibid., 36.

8. White, *The Great Controversy*, 500.

9. Ibid., 499.

10. White, *Patriarchs and Prophets*, 41.

11. Ibid., 36, 37.

12. Ibid.

13. White, *Patriarchs and Prophets*, 39.

14. White, *The Great Controversy*, 496.

15. White, *Patriarchs and Prophets*, 39.

16. Ellen G. White, *The Story of Redemption* (Washington, DC: Review and Herald® Pub. Assn., 1947), 26.

17. White, *Patriarchs and Prophets*, 38.

18. White, *The Great Controversy*, 499.
19. White, *Patriarchs and Prophets*, 33.
20. Ibid., 34.
21. White, *The Story of Redemption*, 29, 30.
22. Ibid., 31.
23. Ibid., 30.
24. Ibid., 32.
25. Ibid., 31.
26. Ibid., 32.
27. Ibid.
28. Ellen G. White, *Education* (Mountain View, CA: Pacific Press® Pub. Assn., 1903), 24.
29. White, *The Story of Redemption*, 33.
30. Ellen G. White, "God's Requirement in Grace, the Same as in Paradise," *Signs of the Times*, May 12, 1890, 274.
31. White, *The Story of Redemption*, 33.
32. White, *The Desire of Ages*, 329, 330.
33. White, *The Great Controversy*, 593, 594.

Dare to Be a Daniel

In the previous chapter, we were introduced to the cosmic controversy in heaven and on planet Earth. This cosmic controversy is the biblical worldview that unfolds from Genesis to Revelation. It is the unchanging context in which the biblical narratives, prophecies, and doctrines are best discerned. Thus, the historicist school of interpretation is found in Scripture, because the history of the cosmic controversy is presented throughout the Bible. This is just one reason why it is important that we read and understand the Bible.

Yet certain books of the Bible can be difficult to comprehend: part of the book of Daniel was sealed until the end time (Daniel 12:4),[1] and some people argue that the book of Revelation is impossible to decipher. But the Bible is a revelation of Jesus Christ and deserves to be comprehended.

To better understand God's Word, we will focus on the man Daniel in this chapter. His role in the cosmic controversy needs to be studied in the light of God's mission to a world in rebellion. Before we begin our study on Daniel, we will briefly review the history of Israel and how Daniel came to be in Babylon.

Preparation for the End Time

The mission of Abraham

Why did God call Abraham out of Ur of the Chaldees in ancient Mesopotamia? It was because his descendants were to bless all the families of the earth (Genesis 12:1–3). In other words, they were to be used to announce to all nations the everlasting gospel's news of a coming Savior and to warn them of Satan's deceptions. This was God's way to counteract the cosmic controversy that caused all humans to sin and to need salvation.

God wanted to use Israel as a great evangelistic avenue to reveal Himself to the world and promised great blessings to His chosen people. He said,

> "If you diligently obey the voice of the LORD your God, to observe carefully all His commandments which I command you today, . . . the LORD your God will set you high above all nations of the earth. . . .
>
> ". . . And the LORD will make you the head and not the tail; you shall be above only, and not be beneath, if you heed the commandments of the LORD your God, which I command you today, and are careful to observe them" (Deutcronomy 28:1, 13, NKJV).

Never before had any nation enjoyed such protections as Israel did during the plagues of Egypt while in the land of Goshen. Never before had a nation been delivered so miraculously as when the greatest army in the world moved in behind Israel and trapped it at the Red Sea. Never before had God defeated enemies for His people in such a way as the Lord did for Israel when it occupied the Promised Land. Never before had God written the law with His own finger, on stone tablets, to guide His people. Never before had the Creator of the universe dwelt with His people in a sanctuary and temple. No nation had been so blessed as Israel.

The Israelites should have seen the obvious difference in how they were treated compared with other nations. But no! They wanted to be like other nations with gods and idols and have a king too (Ezekiel 23:30; 1 Samuel 8:1–22). What blindness they had!

In response to their desire for other gods, God exclaimed,

> "Has a nation ever changed its gods?
>   (Yet they are not gods at all.)
> But my people have exchanged their glorious God
>   for worthless idols" (Jeremiah 2:11; cf. 8:19; 22:9).

Look how far they went. Judah had as many gods as it had towns (verse 28). It had as many altars to Baal as there were streets in Jerusalem (Jeremiah 11:13; cf. 11:17; 19:4, 5; 23:13; 32:29). No wonder God said, "My people have forgotten me, days without number" (Jeremiah 2:32), for Israel had "defiled the land and committed adultery with stone and wood" (Jeremiah 3:9).

The nations of Judah and Israel were full of hypocrisy: "You [God] are always on their lips but far from their hearts" (Jeremiah 12:2). God wasn't their true love; idols had replaced Him. They worshiped heavenly bodies—"the sun, moon and stars" (Acts 7:42; cf. Jeremiah 8:2), as well as Molek and Rephan (Acts 7:43; cf. Leviticus 18:21; 20:2; Jeremiah 32:35). Their "detestable idols" defiled the sacred house of God and His sanctuary (Jeremiah 7:30; Ezekiel 5:11). They burned "incense to Baal and follow[ed] other gods" and made "cakes to offer to the Queen of Heaven" (Jeremiah 7:9, 18; cf. 44:17, 18). In "the entrance of the north gate of the house of the LORD," women mourned for "the god Tammuz" (Ezekiel 8:14), and in "the inner court of the LORD's house . . . were about twenty-five men with their backs toward the temple of the LORD and their faces toward the east, and they . . . [worshiped] the sun toward the east" (verse 16, NKJV). This was spiritual adultery. God pointed out, "They even sacrificed their children, whom they bore to me, as food for them" (Ezekiel 23:37). That's how far the people had distanced themselves from the living, saving God!

Covenant relationship

Deuteronomy 28 begins with an incredible promise for the Israelites—to be above all nations! Many promises follow (verses 2–13), yet they end with these admonitions: "Do not turn aside from any of the commands I will give you today, to the right or to the left, following other gods and serving them" (verse 14). If they turned from God, He would "scatter . . . [them] among all peoples, from one end of the earth to the other. . . . And among those nations . . . [they would] find no rest" (Deuteronomy 28:64, 65, NKJV). But this is exactly what Israel and Judah did, and so they received the curses that God warned of (verses 16–68).

After being scattered among the nations, they had a "despairing heart" and lived in "constant suspense" (verses 64, 66). By breaking the covenant relationship, they ended up as broken nations, disconnected from the Source of life. Their refusal to remain in a loving relationship with God voided the blessings they could have received.

Back in Babylonia

God repeatedly warned His people of the consequences of their wickedness: "From the time your ancestors left Egypt until now, day after day, again and again I sent you my servants the prophets. But they did not listen to me or pay attention. They were stiff-necked and did more evil than their ancestors" (Jeremiah 7:25, 26).

Just consider the kings of Israel and Judah. The twenty kings in Israel were all evil. Even Jehu, who destroyed Baal worship, was like the other kings; he did not turn away from the idolatry of Jeroboam. Of the twenty kings of Judah, thirteen were completely evil, five were not fully dedicated to God, and only two (Hezekiah and Josiah) were good.[2]

Yet these kings weren't the only ones whose hearts were full of iniquity. God said, "Both prophet and priest are godless" (Jeremiah 23:11a); and "priests do violence to my law and profane my holy things; they do not distinguish between the holy and the common; they teach that there is no difference between the unclean and the clean; and they shut their eyes to the keeping of my Sabbaths, so that I am profaned among them" (Ezekiel 22:26). The people—even the priests—had turned from God.

It is no wonder that Israel went into captivity in Assyria and Judah went into captivity in Babylon. Eventually, the northern kingdom of Israel was scattered among many nations and ceased to be a nation. Only Judah was left; and it ended up in Babylon.[3] God had called Abraham to leave Ur, but his descendants were forced to return there. How foolish Israel and Judah had been! Why did they separate from the only true God and worship gods of their own making? No gains were in this—only loss!

But God had a plan (Jeremiah 29:10–14). He worked through individuals to accomplish what was impossible through Israel and Judah. Daniel and his friends, who were taken captive to Babylon, are an outstanding example of this. Let's see how God used them.

God's witnesses

In the book of Daniel, we find faithful followers who are types of those who will be ready for Christ's second advent. The covenant promise God made to Abraham—"all peoples on earth will be blessed" (Genesis 12:3)—is fulfilled through these witnesses, both in the past and in the future. Now let us turn to the man Daniel and his testimony.

The story of Daniel begins as he and his companions come from Judah and receive training in order to serve in the Babylonian court (Daniel 1:6). "Daniel resolved not to defile himself with the royal food and wine, and he asked the chief official for permission not to defile himself this way" (verse 8). Note that Daniel *resolved* and then *asked* for permission. He chose wisely and asked graciously. "Give us nothing but vegetables to eat and water to drink" (verse 12; cf. verse 16). This indicates Daniel's knowledge of God's Edenic diet. In the garden God said, "I give you every seed-bearing plant on the face of the whole earth and every tree that has fruit with seed in it.

They will be yours for food" (Genesis 1:29; cf. 2:16; 3:18). Daniel believed God's Word and acted accordingly.

He knew that the king's food and wine would defile him. Partaking of this food would destroy his discernment. A clear brain (frontal lobe), in tune with God, was vital to Daniel's representing God to the pagans that surrounded him.

What was the result of eating God's diet? "God gave knowledge and understanding of all kinds of literature and learning. And Daniel could understand visions and dreams of all kinds" (Daniel 1:17). Daniel and his three friends put first things first: following God and His plan for living brought His blessing of knowledge and understanding.

God's revelation

Sometime after Daniel's training ended, King Nebuchadnezzar had a dream that he wanted interpreted. But none of his wise men could tell him what he had dreamed. Nebuchadnezzar was furious and shouted, "Execute all the wise men of Babylon!" (see Daniel 2:12). This included Daniel and his three friends (verse 13). Arioch, the commander of the king's guard, went to obey the king's order. "Daniel spoke to him with *wisdom* and *tact*" (verse 14; emphasis added). With permission granted, Daniel entered the throne room and asked the king to give him time to interpret the dream (verse 16). Daniel knew God would help him and enlisted his friends as prayer partners. "He urged them to plead for mercy from the God of heaven" (verse 18a). That night God revealed the king's dream to Daniel in a vision, and Daniel praised God (verses 19–23).

The next morning Daniel stood before the king. He did not focus on himself but gave God the credit. "There is a God in heaven who reveals mysteries. He has shown King Nebuchadnezzar what will happen in days to come" (verse 28). He then showed that God knew the future—foretelling the rise and fall of kingdoms (verses 29–45). In summation, he said, "The great God has shown the king what will take place in the future" (verse 45). The king prostrated himself before Daniel and said,

"Surely your God is the God of gods . . . and a revealer of mysteries" (verse 47).

Counterfeit gods do not know the future and cannot give wisdom and understanding. Only Daniel's God was able to explain the king's dream.

The golden image

Nebuchadnezzar had dreamed of a large statue. "The head of the statue was made of pure gold, its chest and arms of silver, its belly and thighs of bronze, its legs of iron, its feet partly of iron and partly of baked clay" (verse 32). The golden head in the king's dream represented Nebuchadnezzar and his empire; the rest of the statue portrayed subsequent empires. But Nebuchadnezzar was not content with being the golden head. He ordered the construction of a similar statue—made of gold from head to toe—to represent himself. Commanding everyone in his kingdom to worship the image, he exempted no one, not even Daniel's three friends.

Like Daniel, they were different. They refused to worship the golden image, and the king grew furious. In a rage, he demanded, "Make the blazing furnace seven times hotter. No god can rescue you" (see Daniel 3:15, 19). Daniel's friends remained unafraid: "The God we serve is able to deliver us. . . . But even if he does not, . . . we will not serve your gods or worship the image of gold" (verses 17, 18). What courage they had! We need this same faith and moral strength when the death decree is issued in the end time (Revelation 13:15).

Nebuchadnezzar had the three men thrown into a furnace, but he was shocked by what he saw afterward. "Look! I see four men walking around in the fire, unbound and unharmed, and the fourth looks like a son of the gods. . . . Servants of the Most High God, come out" (verses 25, 26). Once outside the furnace, the king inspected them. "The fire had not harmed their bodies, nor was a hair of their heads singed; and there was no smell of fire was on them" (verse 27). Everyone was utterly amazed, and the focus of Nebuchadnezzar was radically changed—no longer was the golden idol the object of his attention but the Living God who stood in the fire and rescued those who worshiped Him. The image of gold stood still, motionless and helpless. Nebuchadnezzar couldn't help praising the Living God and admiring the commitment of Daniel's three friends. "They trusted in him [their God] and defied the king's command and were willing to give up their lives rather than serve or worship any god except their own God" (verse 28). Trust in God alone is crucial. As the three men illustrate, this is how we can prepare for the end-time crisis.

Nebuchadnezzar humbled

Through the witness of Daniel and his three friends, the king knew that only the true God can give and interpret dreams and that He will stand with His own in a fiery furnace and deliver them. Nebuchadnezzar even called Him "the Most High God." But pride hindered him from accepting the Most High God as his God. One day he said, "Is not this the great Babylon I have built as this royal residence, by my mighty power and for the glory of my majesty?" (Daniel 4:30; cf. 5:20). Immediately, a change came over him; the king crawled about fields like an animal and ate grass (Daniel 4:31–33).

After seven years, the king was humbled. He raised his eyes to heaven, and his sanity returned. Nebuchadnezzar had an incredible change of heart. He said,

> I praised the Most High; I honored and glorified him who lives forever.
>
> His dominion is an eternal dominion;
> his kingdom endures from generation to
> generation. . . .
>
> . . . Now I, Nebuchadnezzar, praise and exalt and glorify the King of heaven, because everything he does is right and all his ways are just. And those who walk in pride he is able to humble (verses 34b, 37).

28

Forced worship

Nebuchadnezzar eventually died, and a series of rulers followed him. But ultimately Daniel's prediction of a new empire came true as the Medes and the Persians conquered the Babylonians. The new king, Darius the Mede, was impressed with Daniel and "planned to set him over the whole kingdom" (Daniel 6:3). But jealousy controlled the kingdom's other two administrators and the 120 satraps under Daniel, just as it controlled Lucifer in heaven. Finding Daniel's life to be beyond reproach, they schemed to trap him by a decree of forced false worship, just as there will be in the end time (verses 4–9; see Revelation 13:1–15).

Daniel learned of the decree, but he opened his window toward Jerusalem as usual and prayed three times that day (Daniel 6:10). He didn't close his window and pray unobserved at his bedside. Can you imagine a more jubilant bunch than those administrators and satraps as they strutted on their way to report to the king?

Though filled with regret, the king gave the order for Daniel to be punished. Daniel was thrown into a lions' den. The king said to Daniel, "May your God, whom you serve continually, rescue you!" (verse 16). The king didn't eat or sleep that night. He was restless and worried. At the crack of dawn, the king hurried to the lions' den. In an "anguished voice," he cried out, "Daniel, servant of the living God, has your God, whom you serve continually, been able to rescue you from the lions?" (verse 20).

Daniel replied, "O king, live forever! My God sent His angel and shut the lions' mouths, so that they have not hurt me, because I was found innocent before Him; and also, O king, I have done no wrong before you" (verse 21, NKJV). Darius was overjoyed, ordered Daniel's release, and found no wound on him "because he had trusted in his God" (verse 23). The false accusers were thrown into the den, where the open mouths of the hungry lions waited.

Good news sent out by two kings

King Nebuchadnezzar and King Darius became evangelists. They sent official decrees far and wide to tell what God had done to save Daniel and his three companions and how God had restored Nebuchadnezzar's sanity (Daniel 3:28, 29; 4; 6:25–27). They witnessed about the Living God who saves in the present. These decrees were the first news of God received by the pagans throughout Babylonia and Media-Persia. No other god could have ever done such things. This was radical and good news: there exists a Living God who can save! The news came as an utter surprise. These events proclaimed hope in an otherwise lonely world where unreal gods dominated lives without liberating the people.

These decrees stated that the kingdom of the Living God will last forever and He is just. What powerful testimonies! These pagan kings joined Daniel and his friends in praising the only true God, who loves and died for the whole world (John 3:16, 17; 1 John 2:2). These decrees became a part of God's holy Word. They introduced the Living God to pagans who also became believers and will be in heaven. Thus, these kings did the work that Israel and Judah should have done. God used Daniel and his three friends as primary agents for this evangelism.

Just as Daniel and his friends were witnesses for God, we are also called to share the story of God's love. "Millions upon millions of souls ready to perish, bound in chains of ignorance and sin, have never so much as heard of Christ's love for them. Were our conditions and theirs reversed, what would we desire them to do for us? All this, as far as lies in our power, we are under the most solemn obligation to do for them."[4]

---

1. This sealing included the 1,260-day prophecy (Daniel 7:25; 12:7) and the 2,300-day prophecy (Daniel 8:14), which were to be revealed in the end time (Revelation 10–14). See *Andrews Study Bible* (Berrien Springs, MI: Andrews University Press, 2010), note on Daniel 12:4.

2. Norman R. Gulley, *Systematic Theology*, vol. 2, *God as Trinity* (Berrien Springs, MI: Andrews University Press, 2011), 328.

3. In Scripture, Satan is typified as the king of Babylon (Isaiah 14:4, 12–15).

4. Ellen G. White, "Following Christ," *Review and Herald*, February 29, 1912, 3.

CHAPTER 3

Jesus in Revelation's Throne Room

When one of my Bibles began to fall apart, I removed the books of Daniel and Revelation and attached them together. It was the smallest Bible I had ever owned, but it said so much that is vital for us to know in this end time of human history. These two books of the Bible pull back the curtain on current events to reveal the cosmic controversy as it enters its final pre-Advent culmination.

In fact, these two books provide God's view of what is taking place on planet Earth. They help us to understand the trajectory of present events, particularly the current unification of churches and religions into a worldwide force that will influence history on a global scale.

After poring over these two books, I am convinced that many Christians are at a disadvantage. If they skip the study of Daniel and Revelation, they cannot fully comprehend what is going on behind the scenes in human history. Apocalyptic, or prophetic, study is vital to a full comprehension of what is presently transpiring among churches and where this is headed. Hence, from this perspective, ecclesiology (the theological doctrine of a church) and eschatology (the doctrine of final events) are never fully developed in the theological systems of churches that do not fully take into account the messages of Daniel and

Revelation. This is why the Seventh-day Adventist Church is so fortunate to understand how events are moving toward a global ecclesiastical union that will have the power to persecute commandment keepers (Revelation 13:1–15).

Comparing the books of Daniel and Revelation

The books of Daniel and Revelation are similar, for they are historical, eschatological, and apocalyptic (unveiling). They use symbols, praise the true God, and oppose false gods. Both books ask challenging questions that are directed at God's people: "Who is the god who will deliver you from my hands?" (Daniel 3:15, NKJV). "Who is like the beast? Who is able to make war with him?" (Revelation 13:4, NKJV). Both books include a primarily historical division (Daniel 1–6; Revelation 1–12) and a primarily eschatological division (Daniel 7–12; Revelation 13–22). Both books speak of the resurrected Christ (Daniel 7:13, 14; Revelation 1:10–20). Both books focus on a compromised power that speaks pompous words against God, exists during a 1,260-year period, and persecutes the saints (Daniel 7:6–8, 19–25; Revelation 12:13–16). Both books focus on God's throne in heaven (Daniel 7:9, 10; Revelation 4; 5). Both books have a high regard for God's law (Daniel 7:25; Revelation 12:17; 14:12). Both books speak of a judgment in heaven during the end time, known as the pre-Advent judgment (Daniel 7:9–14; Revelation 14:6, 7). Both books include a command to worship an image or die (Daniel 3:1–28; Revelation 13:14, 15). Both books reveal God's deliverance of His people from human death decrees (Daniel 3:23–27; 6:26, 27; Revelation 19:19–21). Both books offer a blessing (Daniel 12:12; Revelation 22:7). Both books speak of the destruction of the counterfeit church system and the deliverance of God's people. Both books deal with the unfolding and the climax of the cosmic controversy.[1]

Both books' authors—Daniel and John, the writers of Daniel and Revelation respectively—were in captivity when they received divine revelation. Daniel was a captive in Babylon;

John was a prisoner on the Isle of Patmos. Their books, in part, have to do with times when God's people are undergoing persecution. So both books bring encouragement to God's people when dealing with affliction, including the persecution that will occur in the end time. These books remind God's people that He will be with them through it all (Hebrews 13:5; Matthew 28:20) and that just as Christ went through suffering before His triumph and ascension to heaven, so His people in the end time will suffer, triumph, and ascend to heaven in the Second Advent.

Both books show that pride is the hallmark of the enemy of God's people (Daniel 7:8, 11, 20; Revelation 18:7). Pride reflects Satan, whose "heart became proud" (Ezekiel 28:17) and who considered himself God (Isaiah 14:12, 13; cf. Ezekiel 28:2). This reflection is also seen in nations such as Babylon and Moab. Scripture says,

Babylon, . . .
    the pride and glory of the Babylonians,
will be overthrown by God
    like Sodom and Gomorrah (Isaiah 13:19).

We have heard of the pride of Moab—
    how proud he is!—
of his arrogance, his pride, and his insolence;
    in his idle boasting he is not right (Isaiah 16:6,
        ESV).

This is the same pride that we find in Pharaoh and Nebuchadnezzar (Exodus 5:2; Daniel 4:30, 37). Christ has never been proud, even though He is truly God. Philippians 2:6–8 informs us that He laid aside the use of His divinity[2] when He became human: "And being found in appearance as a man, he humbled himself by becoming obedient to death—even death on a cross!" (verse 8). He invites people to follow Him and His example: "Take my yoke upon you and learn from me, for I am gentle and humble in heart, and you will find rest for your souls" (Matthew 11:29). Compared to Christ, pride is shown to be self-centered and un-Christian. "God opposes the proud" (James 4:6)!

Both books indicate that in the time of the end the boasting, persecuting system that is opposed to God will be defeated:

> "He [the little horn; see verses 20, 24] will speak against the Most High and oppress his holy people. . . .
>
> "But the court will sit, and his power will be taken away and completely destroyed forever" (Daniel 7:25, 26).

"Woe! Woe to you, great city, you might city of Babylon! In one hour your doom has come!" (Revelation 18:10).

Like two bookends, Daniel and Revelation tell salvation's story from beginning to end. God's people suffer captivity in ancient Babylon and millennia later are persecuted by the contemporary Babylon the Great. (Later we will establish that the end-time power opposed to God, identified as Babylon, is a religiopolitical [church and state] power with historic roots in the medieval period.)

The story in these two books could be called "A Tale of Two Babylons." The first Babylon is local; the final Babylon is universal. The first Babylon is small; the final Babylon is large. The first Babylon is literal; the final Babylon is spiritual. The first Babylon is a type; the final Babylon is an antitype.

Charged with being the antichrist

In the sixteenth century, the Roman Catholic Church was considered the antichrist by all the Reformers. They based their claim on studying Daniel, 2 Thessalonians 2, and Revelation. With the newly introduced printing press, the views of Protestant leaders such as Martin Luther spread quickly and shook the Roman Catholic Church to its roots. Never before had the papacy been so mightily challenged.

Reeling from this attack, the Roman Catholic Church convened the Council of Trent (1545–1563). It had two major tasks: (1) to destroy the Protestant Reformation, and (2) to deflect a charge of being the antichrist. The latter was done through shifting the antichrist back into the distant past (called *preterism*) or forward into the future (called *futurism*)—both away from the present. They chose futurism.

However, the cosmic controversy is not limited to the early church (preterism), nor is it confined to the end time (futurism). Preterism and futurism are confined either to the past or to the future, whereas the cosmic controversy on planet Earth includes all time from the beginning to the end of human history. So together preterism and futurism include only a small part of history, overlooking the majority of humanity's time and the majority of the cosmic controversy.

Historicist interpretation of Revelation

Revelation presents the cosmic controversy, with Revelation 12 serving as "an overview of history from the birth of Christ to the final events"[3] and as a link between the controversy's history (Revelation 1–11) and future events (Revelation 13–22). For example, the plan of salvation unfolds chronologically from Calvary (Revelation 1:5) to the first apartment of heaven's sanctuary (the seven lampstands and the "golden altar"; Revelation 4:5; 8:3) to the ark of the covenant in the second apartment (Revelation 11:19).[4] Revelation 13–22 discusses those events that were and are still to come.

A careful reading of Revelation shows that the feasts of Israel receive special attention. The festival year included at least five major feasts—the Feasts of Passover, Pentecost, Trumpets, Atonement, and Tabernacles (Leviticus 23). Passover, or Calvary, is the first event mentioned (Revelation 1:5) after the introduction (verses 1–4); and the reference to it is repeated (verses 17, 18). Pentecost (Revelation 4; 5) comes before Trumpets (Revelation 8–11). Those festivals come before the Day of Atonement (Revelation 13–20), which precedes Tabernacles (Revelation 21).

Note that the Feast of Trumpets ends in Revelation 11, just when verse 19 reveals the first view of the ark of the covenant in the Most Holy Place. This means that both the sanctuary furniture and the Jewish feasts in Revelation 1–11 point to the fact that these events take place during the ministry of Christ in the Holy Place (and hence are historical), while the events of Revelation 13–20 happen during the Day of Atonement ministry of Christ in the Most Holy Place (and hence are eschatological).

The postmillennial Feast of Tabernacles concludes the feasts in Revelation as Christ comes to tabernacle with humankind (Revelation 21:1–3). Thus, the sanctuary and festival structures support the historical-eschatological divisions (Revelation 1–11 and 13–22) presented in this chapter.

Heaven's throne

The New Testament repeatedly states that after Christ's ascension He went to the Father and sat down at His right hand on the throne (Mark 16:19; Acts 2:33, 34; 5:31; Romans 8:34; Ephesians 1:20; Colossians 3:1; Hebrews 1:3, 13; 8:1; 10:12; 12:2; 1 Peter 3:22). Some interpreters have concluded that the ascended Christ went into the Most Holy Place where the throne was presumed to be located, even though Revelation 4, 5, and 8 has a throne-room scene, with "bowls full of incense" and the altar of incense (Revelation 5:8; 8:3, 4), in the historical segment of Revelation and thus in the first apartment of the sanctuary. These interpreters overlook the fact that Scripture speaks of movable thrones.

Biblical history and prophecy both mention thrones that were moved. For example, the kings of Israel and Judah sat on movable thrones by the entrance gate to Samaria (2 Chronicles 18:9). In prophecy, wheels represent mobility. Ezekiel and Daniel had visions that included movable thrones. Ezekiel speaks of four cherubim moving wherever the Spirit of God moved (Ezekiel 1:4–12; cf. 10:14). "Above the vault [expanse] over their heads was what looked like a throne of lapis lazuli, and high above on the throne was a figure like that of a man" (Ezekiel 1:26). Wheels are mentioned in connection with this movable throne (verses 15–17).[5] Just as God's presence in the earthly sanctuary and temple was not confined to the Most Holy Place, so the throne in heaven moved from the first apartment into the second (Exodus 33:9; Ezekiel 9:3). Daniel saw this while in vision:

"Thrones were set in place,
    and the Ancient of Days took his seat.
His clothing was as white as snow. . . .
His throne was flaming with fire,
    and its wheels were all ablaze.
A river of fire was flowing,
    coming out from before him" (Daniel 7:9, 10).

Throne-room scenes

The word *throne* (Greek *thronos*) occurs sixty-one times in the New Testament. Forty-five of these occurrences are in the book of Revelation.[6] There are seven throne-room, or temple, scenes in Revelation that introduce new sections (Revelation 4–5; 8:2–6; 11:19; 15; 16:17–17:3; 19:1–10; 21:5–11).

The throne-room scenes are shown prior to the things that happen on earth because God wants people to fix their hearts on events in heaven—the control center of the universe—and then face the problems on earth. This focus enables Christ's followers to deal triumphantly with the crises on earth by giving them encouragement and hope. Looking to Christ and studying His word provides them with strength and courage as they prepare for the final crisis.

1. The book of Daniel is the primary Old Testament foundation for the book of Revelation.

2. *Andrews Study Bible*, note on Philippians 2:7.

3. *Andrews Study Bible*, note on Revelation 12:1–7.

4. *Andrews Study Bible*, note on Revelation 11:19.

5. *Andrews Study Bible*, note on Ezekiel 1:16.

6. Mark Driscoll, "The Church and the Supremacy of Christ in a Postmodern World," in *The Supremacy of Christ in a Postmodern World*, eds. John Piper and Justin Taylor (Wheaton, IL: Crossway Books, 2007), 131.

CHAPTER 4

Salvation and Hope

In this chapter, we will focus on the love of the Trinity and our assurance of salvation. We will look at the terrible price it cost the Trinity to save us and ensure our salvation, giving us hope for the present and the future.

The Trinity

The Trinity are eternal. They never had a beginning. There never was a time when They didn't know about the coming cosmic controversy. Hence, there never was a time when They didn't know of the terrible anguish, the criminal treatment from vile wretches, and the enormous weight of human sin that would crush out the life of Christ. But They had a plan in place. When sin entered the universe, the Trinity had to put it into action, even though it was an enormous price to pay: Jesus would become fully God and fully man to save humans from sin.

It took a God-man to save humans

When God became man, two natures were joined together. The divinity of God and the humanity of the human race formed a unique God-man unlike any other individual throughout the universe. Never before and never again will there be another Person like Jesus Christ. He became a very small presence in Mary and remained in her for nine months. Humans will never understand this divine mystery.

Our utter inability to comprehend this mystery is like an ant attempting to understand Einstein's theories of relativity. It's impossible. While there was no hint of sin in Christ, He had to be human in order to live a human life and to form a perfect human character and provide a perfect sacrifice. His humanity allowed Him to understand the human experience and sympathize with a suffering world (Hebrews 4:14–16; 5:7–9).

Salvation in the Old and New Testaments

While Christ's sacrifice took place in the New Testament, God's forgiving and saving power was available from the beginning of human history and has continued on through time (Micah 7:18, 19; cf. Isaiah 61:10). This means that the God of law in the Old Testament is no different from the God of grace in the New Testament because salvation embraces forgiveness for lawbreaking whenever needed throughout history—this is grace. No wonder then that the Old Testament God was called a God of awesome grace (Exodus 34:6, 7; Psalm 86:15; Joel 2:13).

Although the sacrifices in the Old Covenant couldn't take away sins, or lawbreaking (1 John 3:4), the Savior could take away sins (Hebrews 10:1–14). "As far as the east is from the west, so far has he removed our transgressions from us" (Psalm 103:12) because He is "to Israel a forgiving God" (Psalm 99:8; cf. Jeremiah 50:20; Ezekiel 18:22). He deals with sins the same way in both covenants on the basis of His future or past payment for sins at Calvary (Isaiah 53:5).

The plan of salvation is therefore the same throughout history because God does not change: "From everlasting to everlasting you are God"; "Jesus Christ is the same yesterday and today and forever" (Psalm 90:2; Hebrews 13:8; cf. Malachi 3:6). The gospel was preached to Abraham (Galatians 3:8) and to the nation of Israel (Hebrews 4:6) and is called the "eternal gospel" (Revelation 14:6).

But why did Jesus Christ, "the Lamb who was slain from the creation of the world" (Revelation 13:8), need to die? Because the "wages of sin is death"—nothing less (Romans 6:23). If Christ died for lawbreaking and sin's wages could have been paid in any other way, then Christ's death was a huge mistake.

Christ's human life
No human ever lived under so difficult a mission as Christ: just one sin would have dashed the hopes of human salvation and would have forever separated Him from the Godhead. While He went about His mission on Earth, the Jewish leaders plotted to trap and kill Him and dogged His footsteps during His public work. And above all, Satan and his demonic fiends never ceased to harass Him. Despite this, Christ came to live a human life at its lowest in order to empathize with the worst of sinners and the most desperate of addicts.

Gethsemane
During much of His life, Jesus knew He would die, and this caused Him great concern. "I have a baptism to undergo, and what constraint I am under until it is completed" (Luke 12:50). By the time He was in Gethsemane, Christ "felt that by sin He was being separated from His Father. The gulf was so broad, so black, so deep, that His spirit shuddered before it. [In] this agony He must not exert His divine power to escape. As man He must suffer the consequences of man's sin."[1]

"Satan told Him that if He became the surety for a sinful world, the separation would be eternal."[2] He was "seized with superhuman agony . . . fainting and exhausted. . . . 'His sweat was as it were great drops of blood falling down to the ground.' "[3] "The humanity of the Son of God trembled in that trying hour."[4]

Christ's prayers in Gethsemane express His horror and deep heart-rending anguish as never before. The Sin Bearer pleaded with His Father for release from His mission, if it were possible. He was "deeply distressed and troubled" and exclaimed,

" 'My soul is overwhelmed with sorrow to the point of death.' . . . Going a little farther, he fell to the ground," indicating that the anguish He carried was a crushing load (Mark 14:33–35). Three times He shrank from His mission (verses 34–41) but added three times "not as I will, but as you will" (Matthew 26:39, 42, 44; cf. Mark 14:36, Luke 22:42). He had come to do His Father's will (Hebrews 10:5–7). As Ellen White put it, Christ decided He would "save man at any cost to Himself."[5]

Trials

No one was so horribly treated as our Savior. In His trial before Annas, "Christ suffered keenly under abuse and insult. At the hands of the beings whom He had created, and for whom He was making an infinite sacrifice, He received every indignity. . . . His trial by men who acted as fiends was to Him a perpetual sacrifice. To be surrounded by human beings under the control of Satan was revolting to Him. And He knew that in a moment, by the flashing forth of His divine power, He could lay His cruel tormentors in the dust. This made the trial harder to bear."[6]

The Sanhedrin decided Christ should die, but such a decision at night was against Jewish law.

> In legal condemnation nothing could be done except in the light of day and before a full session of the council. Notwithstanding this, the Saviour was now treated as a condemned criminal, and given up to be abused by the lowest and vilest of humankind. . . . While in the guardroom, awaiting His legal trial, He was not protected. The ignorant rabble had seen the cruelty with which He was treated before the council, and from this they took license to manifest all the satanic elements of their nature. Christ's very nobility and godlike bearing goaded them to madness. His meekness, His innocence, His majestic patience, filled them with hatred born of Satan. Mercy and justice were trampled upon.

Never was [a] criminal treated in so inhuman a manner as was the Son of God.[7]

Later in Herod's court, Christ remained silent to the demands that He prove His divinity. With passionate anger, Herod yelled at Him:

If You are an impostor [or are not willing to prove Your divinity], death at their [the multitude's] hands is only what You merit; if You are the Son of God, save Yourself by working a miracle.

No sooner were these words spoken than a rush was made for Christ. Like wild beasts, the crowd darted upon their prey. Jesus was dragged this way and that, Herod joining the mob in seeking to humiliate the Son of God. Had not the Roman soldiers interposed, and forced back the maddened throng, the Saviour would have been torn in pieces.[8]

Finally, back in Pilate's court, "Jesus was taken, faint with weariness and covered with wounds, and scourged in the sight of the multitude."[9] Then the soldiers clothed Him with purple, shoved a crown of thorns on His head, and harassed Him, calling, "Hail, king of the Jews!" They spit at Him. "A maddened throng" surrounded the Savior of the world. "Mocking and jeering" filled the air, along with "coarse oaths of blasphemy." Christ's "lowly birth and humble life" and "His claim to be the Son of God" were discussed and derided by the mob, and "the vulgar jest and insulting sneer . . . [were] passed from lip to lip."[10]

In His terrible trials, and even before, Christ was "mocked and rejected. There [in Jerusalem] the waves of mercy, still returning in a stronger tide of love, had been beaten back by hearts as hard as a rock."[11] He permitted Satan and his fiends the freedom to harass, mock, and murder Him. While lavish love flowed from Christ, utter hatred controlled the devil and his demon-possessed wretches. These attributes vividly reveal and expose the contrary sides of the cosmic controversy. Oh, what a wonderful Savior we have that He was willing to undergo such trials for us!

Calvary

After being sentenced to crucifixion, Christ was nailed to a cross that was dropped into a hole, wrenching His flesh in anguish. His lacerated back, ripped to shreds after His earlier scourging, was raw and bloody as He heaved forward for breath on the cross, only to fall back onto the rough wood in agony (Matthew 27:26). He hung there to save all humans, including the wretches that tortured Him (1 John 2:2). He hung there to forgive you and me. What a wonderful God!

He hung there in torturous pain, yet far greater than the pain was the guilt of the world that crushed the life out of His sinless mind and heart. Never will created beings comprehend the magnitude of the guilt He bore in our place: "Heaven viewed with grief and amazement Christ hanging upon the cross, blood flowing from His wounded temples. . . . His labored breath grew quick and deep, as His soul panted under the burden of the sins of the world."[12] He bore my guilt and yours.

It cost Him everything to save us. The price of sin was so great that it disconnected the Trinity—as He who knew no sin became sin for us (2 Corinthians 5:21)—for sin separates (Isaiah 59:2). This is why Christ cried out loudly on the cross: "My God, my God, why have you forsaken me?" (Matthew 27:46).

Yet God hadn't forsaken Christ on the cross; the crushing weight of human sin separated Him from the Father and the Holy Spirit. The Father and the Holy Spirit anguished over the extreme suffering Christ endured in His final days. Their hearts were wrenched by His agony. "God was in Christ reconciling the world to Himself" (2 Corinthians 5:19, NKJV).

The sinless Christ not only suffered as one sinner who was lost but as all sinners. He took the place of all the billions of humans throughout human history. Not just one sin but multiplied trillions of sins—all sins—were heaped upon Him, so He seemed to be hopelessly lost.

Slowly the hours passed as He hung helplessly on the cross. Finally, He cried, "It is finished" (John 19:30). What a cry! After an arduous battle of many years, His mission was accomplished! Christ conquered! His victory impacted every created being throughout unnumbered worlds: "To the angels and the unfallen worlds the cry, 'It is finished,' had a deep significance. It was for them as well as for us that the great work of redemption had been accomplished. They with us share the fruits of Christ's victory."[13] Oh, what matchless love! You can't help loving Him forever!

Yet the story of redemption does not end with Jesus' death. Christ was raised from the dead! He had said, "I lay down My life that I may take it again. No one takes it from Me, but I lay it down of Myself. I have power to lay it down, and I have power to take it again" (John 10:17, 18, NKJV). It was Christ's choice to die for humans and to rise again to intercede for them in the heavenly sanctuary.

Christ's promise of the Holy Spirit

Christ promised that after He ascended to heaven "another Helper" would come to His disciples (John 14:16, NKJV). This Helper (NKJV; ESV), also called "another advocate" (NIV) or "another Comforter" (KJV), is the Holy Spirit, who is more than an influence. In fact, He is "the Third Person of the Godhead," just as Christ is the Second Person of the Godhead.[14] The Holy Spirit is a Person with functions to fulfill in the cosmic controversy, just as Christ had functions in the Godhead to fulfill. "The Holy Spirit is Christ's representative, but divested of the personality of humanity and independent thereof. Cumbered with humanity, Christ could not be in every place personally. Therefore it was for their [the disciples'] interest that He should go to the Father, and send the Spirit to be His successor on earth."[15]

Let's unpack this statement.

1. Christ and the Holy Spirit are two different Persons.
2. They are both Persons in the Godhead.
3. One function of the Holy Spirit since Pentecost is to be Christ's successor on earth.
4. But the Holy Spirit does not add to the saving work of Christ.
5. This is because the Holy Spirit applies Christ's completed sacrificial atonement to the lives of Christ's followers (Romans 8:11, 14).
6. The Holy Spirit convicts the world of sin, righteousness, and judgment of Satan. He guides people into all truth, based on Scripture, which He inspired (John 16:8–13; 2 Peter 1:21).
7. Thus, there is only one Savior, Jesus Christ, even though all Three Members of the Godhead love the world, and Each contributes to the plan of salvation.
8. Just as Christ brought glory to the Father, the Holy Spirit brings glory to Christ, and the Father brings glory to Christ (John 17:4; 16:14; 17:1, 22, 24).

It takes the Third Person of the Godhead to be the successor of Christ—the Second Person of the Godhead—on earth. This is because Christ ascended to the heavenly sanctuary to minister on our behalf, which we will discuss in the next chapter.

The gospel

This study of Christ's sacrifice helps us glimpse what He went through to save us, and two verses capture His offer of salvation: "Come to me, all you who are weary and burdened, and I will give you rest. Take my yoke upon you and learn from me, for I am gentle and humble in heart, and you will find rest for your souls. For my yoke is easy and my burden is light" (Matthew 11:28–30). The second is,

"Remain in me, as I also remain in you. No branch can bear fruit by itself; it must remain in the vine. Neither can you bear fruit unless you remain in me.

Salvation and Hope

"I am the vine; you are the branches. . . . Apart from me you can do nothing" (John 15:4, 5).

Accepting the gift assures us of eternal life, peace in the present, and hope for the future.

-----

1. White, *The Desire of Ages*, 686.
2. Ibid., 687.
3. Ibid., 689.
4. Ibid., 690.
5. Ibid., 693.
6. Ibid., 700.
7. Ibid., 710.
8. Ibid., 731.
9. Ibid., 734.
10. Ibid.
11. Ibid., 829.
12. Ibid., 760.
13. Ibid., 758.
14. Ibid., 671.
15. Ibid., 669.

CHAPTER 5

Jesus Christ as King-Priest

During Jesus' crucifixion, the angry chief priests protested the writing Pilate had put on Jesus' cross, telling Pilate: "Do not write 'The King of the Jews,' but that this man claimed to be king of the Jews" (John 19:21). But this was not the case for Christ's reception in heaven. God the Father welcomed Him: "Your throne, O God, will last for ever and ever" (Hebrews 1:8). God calls Him an enthroned King! What a radical difference! Back home in heaven, away from the horrendous torture He endured from the murderous mob, He was recognized for what He is: "Lord of lords and King of kings" (Revelation 17:14).

Jesus Christ is King-Priest

"The LORD is our king" (Isaiah 33:22). Zechariah predicted that Christ would "be a priest on his throne" (Zechariah 6:13), and His inauguration as King-Priest is presented in Hebrews 1:8–13 and Revelation 4–5. Christ "was designated by God to be high priest in the order of Melchizedek" (Hebrews 5:10). Melchizedek, a type of Jesus, was a king-priest during the time of Abraham (Genesis 14:18; Psalm 110:4; Hebrews 5:6, 10; 7:1–3, 15–17). Note the many times Scripture declares that since Christ's ascension He is seated at God's right hand: Mark

16:19; Acts 2:33–35; 5:31; 7:55, 56; Romans 8:34; Ephesians 1:20–23; Colossians 3:1; Hebrews 1:1–3; 1 Peter 3:22. Christ as King-Priest is seated with God the Father on the throne in the sanctuary of heaven.

Christ's sacrifice gives Him the right to minister as our Priest in heaven, for none can minister without a sacrifice (Hebrews 8:3). Christ's sacrifice on the cross completed the first phase of His ministry, while His subsequent ministries occur in heaven. Redemption took place on the cross, while representation and restoration take place in heaven. "But when this priest had offered for all time one sacrifice for sins, he sat down at the right hand of God" (Hebrews 10:12). No mention is made of the need for other priests or a repetition of the sacrifice: "We have been made holy through the sacrifice of the body of Jesus Christ once for all" (verse 10). Christ's death was just as unique as His incarnation and just as unrepeatable. Christ's high-priestly ministry adds nothing to the Cross, nor does it imply that Christ's sacrifice was insufficient or incomplete (Hebrews 9:24–28). Rather, the ministry brings the benefits of Calvary to humans.

Inauguration of the King-Priest
After His resurrection, Christ briefly visited heaven. He went to the Father in person.

> Jesus refused to receive the homage of His people until He had the assurance that His sacrifice was accepted by the Father. He ascended to the heavenly courts, and from God Himself heard the assurance that His atonement for the sins of men had been ample, that through His blood all might gain eternal life. The Father ratified the covenant made with Christ, that He would receive repentant and obedient men, and would love them even as He loves His Son. Christ was to complete His work, and fulfill His pledge to "make a man more precious than fine gold; even a man than the golden wedge of Ophir." Isaiah 13:12.[1]

Christ spent forty days on earth between His resurrection and ascension (Acts 1:3). Except for His brief trip to the Father, He had been away from heaven for more than thirty years. He was still the Second Person of the Godhead, but He was also the God-man. In Him was a new reality: He was not only God but also Man. In Him, the human race is elevated to be the sons and daughters of God.

Elevation and authority of Jesus Christ

Christ is unique in His authority and is the only one designated by God to exercise it. No one else is qualified, nor is any church.

- "In the past God spoke to our ancestors through the prophets at many times and in various ways, but in these last days he has spoken to us by his Son, whom he appointed heir of all things, and through whom also he made the universe. The Son is the radiance of God's glory and the exact representation of his being, sustaining all things by his powerful word" (Hebrews 1:1–3).
- Christ ascended to heaven, and God the Father said to Him: "Your throne, O God, is forever and ever; a scepter of righteousness is the scepter of Your kingdom" (verse 8, NKJV).
- God "raised Christ from the dead and seated him at his right hand in the heavenly realms, far above all rule and authority, power and dominion, and every name that is invoked, not only in the present age but also in the one to come. And God placed all things under his feet and appointed him to be head over everything for the church, which is his body, the fullness of him who fills everything in every way" (Ephesians 1:20–23).
- "Angels, authorities and powers [are] in submission to him" (1 Peter 3:22).
- Christ said, "All authority in heaven and on earth has been given to me" (Matthew 28:18).
- "Since, then, you [His followers] have been raised with

Christ, set your hearts on things above, where Christ is, seated at the right hand of God" (Colossians 3:1).

This signifies that the only means of salvation is not a church on earth but Christ who ministers for humans in heaven's sanctuary. He is the only qualified High Priest in the Christian era (Hebrews 4:14–16; 7:24–26).[2]

God never intended the church to be the means of salvation for its members. The risen Christ is the God-man in charge of bestowing the gift of His salvation through the Spirit (John 3:5–8; Titus 3:5–7); this is a work never entrusted to humans or to a church, for it is a re-creative work (the divine work of sanctification) that only the Creator God can accomplish. Peter, referring to Christ, said, "Salvation is found in no one else, for there is no other name under heaven given to mankind by which we must be saved" (Acts 4:12). Christ is the only Savior of humans, the only Mediator between humans and God (see 1 Timothy 2:5). Christ said, "I am the way and the truth and the life. No one comes to the Father except through me" (John 14:6).

Because we have the only authorized High Priest on our side, we should not worry about final events on planet Earth, when nearly the whole world will worship Satan. No end-time decree should concern us (Revelation 13:1–15). Christ allows Satan to expose his rebellion, but Christ is in control. Resting in Him alone fits us for heaven.

Inauguration of Christ

John, one of Christ's disciples, had a revelation of Christ years after His ascension to heaven's sanctuary. In this vision, no one was found worthy to open the scroll of history, and John wept.

Then one of the elders said to me, "Do not weep! See, the Lion of the tribe of Judah, the Root of David, has triumphed. He is able to open the scroll and its seven seals."

Then I saw a Lamb, looking as if it had been slain,

standing at the center of the throne (Revelation 5:5, 6).

There He was, the risen Savior, with the marks of His crucifixion indicating His unique authority to take charge of unfolding human history. Then the four living creatures and humans burst into rapturous song:

> "You are worthy to take the scroll
>   and to open its seals,
> because you were slain,
>   and with your blood you purchased for God
>   persons from every tribe and language and people
>   and nation" (verse 9).

Here the Victor at Calvary is inaugurated to sit on God's throne as the Ruler of human history.

As such, Christ is in control of human history as He opens the seals of the scroll, even though it may not look like it to humans in the trenches on earth. Christ allows Satan to reveal his anger and deception in the cosmic controversy, but ultimately Christ remains in control of events on planet Earth. In the end, good will triumph over evil.

We can move forward with courage. We are on the winning side. Christ our Savior works for us in heaven's sanctuary. He works to defeat Satan in our lives. He works to fit us for heaven. He works to give us assurance that we are saved, safe in His strong arms of love that are wrapped around us on our pilgrim journey.

The heavenly sanctuary

The heavenly sanctuary is the original tabernacle, of which the earthly tabernacle and temples were copies (Hebrews 8:5). Although the temples were larger than the tabernacle, each one had the same Holy Places (Exodus 26:33; 28:29; Leviticus 4: 7–30; 6:25–30) and Most Holy Places (Exodus 26:33, 34; Leviticus 16:2–34). This is the most important part of God's specifications. There are two rooms (Holy and Most Holy) for two ministries. Christ's two present ministries in heaven's sanctuary have to do with redemption and restoration, respectively. (We focus on the redemption work in this chapter and will concentrate on the restoration part in chapter 8, when we study the first angel's message.) The first ministry is the daily ministry. The second ministry is the yearly ministry, or Day of Atonement. The daily ministry is continued during the Day of Atonement.

Calvary was the price paid for salvation, for God is holy and sin is abhorrent to Him. Calvary was the gift given to humans because God is love. The holiness and love of God met at the Cross, for Calvary's love is holy love. But Calvary alone is not the whole story of God's grace. Christ's ministry in heaven applies the merits of His death on the cross (Hebrews 10:11–18).

Intercession of the King-Priest

Christ's forgiveness of sins is the same throughout history. Consider Old Testament times. The prophet Zechariah speaks of

> Joshua the high priest standing before the Angel of the LORD, and Satan standing at his right hand to oppose him. And the LORD said to Satan, "The LORD rebuke you, Satan! . . . Is this [man] not a brand plucked from the fire?"
>
> Now Joshua was clothed with filthy garments, and was standing before the Angel.
>
> Then He answered and spoke to those who stood before Him, saying, "Take away the filthy garments from him." And to him He said, "See, I have removed your iniquity from you, and I will clothe you with rich robes" (Zechariah 3:1–4, NKJV).

Clearly, the "eternal gospel" is just the same in the Old Testament as it is in the New (Revelation 14:6). The eternal gospel is also the same in that Christ's power gives the sinner victory over sin. The present era has one difference, but that doesn't change the gospel: Jesus Christ in His present ministry of forgiveness is the God-man. He has lived a perfect human life and intercedes for humans because He understands our humanity.

Scripture says, "During the days of Jesus' life on earth, he offered up prayers and petitions with fervent cries and tears to the one who could save him from death, and he was heard because of his reverent submission. Son though he was, he learned obedience from what he suffered and, once made perfect, he became the source of eternal salvation for all who obey him and was designated by God to be high priest in the order of Melchizedek" (Hebrews 5:7–10). Because of His life on earth, He can empathize with those who pray to Him. Christ "had to be made like them [his brothers], fully human in every way, in order that he might become a merciful and faithful high priest in service to God, and that he might make atonement for the sins of the people. Because he himself suffered when he was tempted, he is able to help those who are being tempted" (Hebrews 2:17, 18).

In the Incarnation, Christ "took the nature of man in its fallen state, bearing the consequences of sin, not its sinfulness. He was one with the human race, except in sin."[3] He received the weakness but not the wickedness of human nature. No wonder the key word of the book of Hebrews is *better*. "For we do not have a high priest who is unable to empathize with our weaknesses, but we have one who has been tempted in every way, just as we are—yet he did not sin. Let us then approach God's throne of grace with confidence, so that we may receive mercy and find grace to help us in our time of need" (Hebrews 4:15, 16). Christ "is able to save completely those who come to God through him, because he always lives to intercede for them" (Hebrews 7:25).

The greatest proof that Christ loves humans is His life and death for them. As the God-man, He can relate to the problem of sin. That is why, after His life and death, Christ is given control of human history (Revelation 5:5) and is made the judge in the final judgments (John 5:27; Revelation 19:14–21).

55

Look up, fellow pilgrim! Look up to Christ on the throne! "Fix your thoughts on Jesus" (Hebrews 3:1). Let Him carry you all the way home, as the shepherd carries the lost sheep (Luke 15:3–7). Let Him bear your burdens, your worries, and your daily trials. Only Christ can carry you through the end time and into heaven.

---

1. White, *The Desire of Ages*, 790.

2. Christ is the only One qualified to serve as Mediator even though all Christ's followers are a "royal priesthood" (1 Peter 2:9), just as in the Old Covenant God's people were a "kingdom of priests" (Exodus 19:6).

3. General Conference of Seventh-day Adventists, Ministerial Association, *Seventh-day Adventists Believe*, 2nd ed. (Nampa, ID: Pacific Press® Pub. Assn., 2005), 56.

CHAPTER 6

Satan's Attack Against God's Law

While in heaven, at God's throne in the sanctuary, Lucifer "began to insinuate doubts concerning the laws that governed heavenly beings, intimating that though laws might be necessary for the inhabitants of the worlds, angels, being more exalted, needed no such restraint, for their own wisdom was a sufficient guide."[1]

"While claiming for himself perfect loyalty to God, he [Lucifer] urged that changes in the order and laws of heaven were necessary for the stability of the divine government."[2] But to question God's law is to question His rule, because His rule is based upon His law. It also questions God's wisdom and His character, for God's law is "the law that gives freedom" (James 2:12).

God's law in heaven

Ellen White tells us that "before this earth was called into being, God's law existed."[3] Yet the Ten Commandments were not written out in heaven. It was irrelevant to speak of honoring one's father and mother, rejecting adultery, and keeping the seventh-day Sabbath. But later, while on Earth, Christ explained the principles that were applicable in heaven: loving God and loving others (Mark 12:30, 31). These same eternal principles are relevant to created beings wherever they are.

But Satan's rebellion opposed these basic truths. He hated God and had no love for anyone. After bearing with Satan's deception and scheming for a lengthy period, God said that Satan had gone too far in his rebellion to return to loyalty. But the angels who followed him had not crossed the line of no return. They were "blinded by his deceptions. To them the counsel and entreaties of the loyal angels opened a door of hope; and had they heeded the warning, they might have broken away from the snare of Satan. But pride, love for their leader, and the desire for unrestricted freedom were permitted to bear sway, and the pleadings of divine love and mercy were finally rejected."[4] The misled angels loved their leader, but Satan had no love for them. Satan's deceptive snare evidently promised them unrestricted freedom, but it hid the fact that crossing the line would bring an abrupt end to their freedom. Never again would these angels be able to love or be loved in return. They were imprisoned for life in the grip of a tyrant. The prison door was forever locked; the keys thrown away. They live a wretched and miserable existence. He loved himself, but he couldn't care less for his captives.

Would you want to join that side of the controversy and lose the ultimate joy and freedom of fellowship with Christ who died to save you? Don't be deceived; the other side has nothing worthwhile to offer. Fitness for heaven is a gift through Jesus Christ, who dearly loves you and wants to save you from the devil's deceptive plans. The Ten Commandments are important because through them Christ guides you to keep loving God and others, which is fitness for heaven. Christ writes these principles in your mind and heart (Jeremiah 31:33; Hebrews 8:10; 10:16). Christ in you is "the hope of glory" (Colossians 1:27).

"Not under the law, but under grace"

Some theologians believe God gave the law in the Old Testament but grace in the New Testament. For example, the theologian Herman Bavinck declared, "Now, in the New Testament,

the law has been fulfilled in Christ. It therefore no longer regulates the holiness relationship that exists between God and his
people. Now Christ has come in the place of the law; in and
through him God regulates the relationship between him and
his people."[5]

If this refers to the ceremonial sacrifices that pointed to
Christ's sacrifice, then Christ did fulfill those laws. But Christ
did not fulfill or replace the moral law. Instead, He said, "Until
heaven and earth disappear, not the smallest letter, not the
least stroke of the pen, will by any means disappear from the
Law" (Matthew 5:18).

Paul wrote to the Romans: "You are not under the law, but
under grace" (Romans 6:14). Paul is saying that we are not
under the law as a means of salvation but under grace—the
only means of salvation. But many Christians believe that
Christ's followers in the Old Testament were under the law,
while His followers since Calvary are under grace. Further-
more they state that the law was done away with at the cross.
This seems to suggest that salvation in the Old Testament was
through works of the law, whereas since Calvary salvation is
through grace.

There are a couple of major problems with this thinking: (1)
it suggests two separate plans of salvation, and (2) it suggests
that the God of the Old Testament is different from the God
of the New Testament. This gives the impression that God
changes and that He doesn't treat His followers the same in the
Old and the New Testament periods. This questions His fair-
ness, which is sufficient enough for Satan to win his case
against God's justice in the cosmic controversy.

But Scripture is clear: "Jesus Christ is the same yesterday
and today and forever" (Hebrews 13:8). This is why the Bible
refers to the "eternal gospel" (Revelation 14:6), for God does
not change (see Malachi 3:6). In the Christian era, because of
Calvary in the past, Christ intercedes as an Advocate for
humans in heaven's sanctuary (Hebrews 7:24–26). But Job,
because of the Calvary to come, could also say in the Old Testament, "Even now my witness is in heaven; my advocate is on

high. My intercessor is my friend" (Job 16:19, 20).

There is a change in the *name* of the covenants when we come to the old and new covenant historical periods but not a change in *nature*. To put it another way, there is a change from the priestly ministry in the earthly sanctuary or temple (old covenant), with its sacrifices and services, to the priestly ministry of the ascended Christ in heaven's sanctuary (new covenant). But the earthly and heavenly ministries both focus on the one unchanging Savior Jesus Christ.

The gospel and its covenant invitation are given to law breakers to bring them to Christ, who died to atone for them and save them. The atonement sacrifice took place on the cross—the only way to pay for law-breaking and to uphold the need for law-keeping. The law does not save but leads us to the Savior to be justified by faith (Galatians 3:21, 24). "Is the law, therefore, opposed to the promises of God? Absolutely not!" (verse 21). That is why Christ said, "If you love me, you will keep my commandments" (John 14:15, ESV). It's a relational promise.

The law's function is to reveal our condition as sinners. The law shows us our need of grace. This is the law's same function throughout history. Law and grace belong together as a part of the eternal gospel. If there has been no law since Calvary, then there has been no need of grace either.

But we need to go deeper and ask why Christ needed to die. He died to pay the enormous debt caused by human sin. In other words, He died to atone for all law-breaking (1 John 3:4). Sin, or law-breaking, and grace met at the cross in Christ's death. If there has been no law since the cross, there has been no law-breaking since then either (which is obviously not true). The law and grace are as inseparable as Christ's divinity and humanity; it was the God-man who hung on the cross. This was the greatest revelation of grace poured out for law-breaking.

It is crucial that we understand God's nature as well as the purpose of Calvary: Christ died to do for us that which we could never do for ourselves—earn salvation for ourselves and demonstrate the utter futility of trying to save ourselves. In dying, Christ not only paid the price for law-breaking but demonstrated the importance of God's unchanging law. In a saving relationship with Christ, forgiven sinners gladly keep His law, through His help, in gratitude for the gift of salvation.

When abiding in Christ, law-keeping is a relationship with Christ that also brings benefits (John 15). This is true throughout salvation's history. This is why the preincarnate Christ said to Israel, "Oh, that they had such a heart in them that they would fear Me and always keep all My commandments, that it might be well with them and with their children forever!" (Deuteronomy 5:29, NKJV). For the Lawgiver is the Redeemer: both the law and grace come from Him and are embedded in the gospel. There is no gospel without the law and grace. If there is no law, then grace isn't necessary.

We now come to a crucial point. The Lord speaks of foreigners and "eunuchs who keep my Sabbaths" in "my covenant," for "my house will be called a house of prayer for all nations" (Isaiah 56:4, 7). Here is the fulfillment of the Abrahamic covenant promise that "all peoples on earth will be blessed through you [Abraham]" (Genesis 12:3; cf. Psalm 72:17). God invites all nations into His covenant, with its Sabbath, which was given to all humans at the end of Creation week (Mark 2:27; Genesis 2:1–3). Jeremiah speaks of this new covenant as necessary because the people broke the old covenant (Jeremiah 31:32). The new covenant was not given in order to write the law in their minds and hearts (verse 33) because the law was written already in the minds and hearts of the true saints in the old covenant (Deuteronomy 6:5, 6; Isaiah 51:7). The first covenant wasn't a trial run on God's part, followed up by an improved attempt called the new covenant. The fault was not with God but with the people (Hebrews 8:8, 9).

The day of the Sabbath

Over the centuries since Christ's death and resurrection, most Christians have come to believe that only the fourth commandment of God's law has changed. They consider Sabbath rest as important but see no reason to keep Saturday holy.

These people overlook two things: First, Christ chose the seventh day, which He blessed and made holy, and not one of the other six days. In the Old Testament, the preincarnate Christ chose the seventh day as the Sabbath at Creation (Genesis 2:2, 3). Later the preincarnate Christ wrote the Ten Commandments with His finger on stone, meaning they are permanent and immutable (Exodus 31:18; 34:28; Deuteronomy 5:22; 10:2, 4). Finally, the Ten Commandments were housed in the ark of the covenant, which was God's throne on earth (Exodus 25:16). They are the basis of His rule.

Second, Christ spent much of His time teaching how to keep the seventh-day Sabbath. The Jewish leaders had loaded it down with so many regulations that it was the worst day of the week. Surely Christ would not have gone to all that effort if He wanted the day to be changed soon in honor of His resurrection. Christ taught the *way* the Sabbath should be kept, not a different *day* to be kept.

In addition, there is no evidence in Scripture for Sunday replacing Saturday. There is evidence of the continuance of Saturday as God's Sabbath. (See Matthew 24:20.)

The Sabbath-Sunday debate during the Reformation

God launched the Protestant Reformation in 1517 when Martin Luther's Ninety-Five Theses questioned the human traditions of the Catholic Church. Thirteen years later the Lutheran Augsburg Confession was written. It is the defining document to distinguish Protestantism from Catholicism.

Among other statements, the confession says, "They [the Roman Catholic papacy] allege the change of the Sabbath into the Lord's day, contrary, as it seemeth, to the Decalogue. . . . They will needs have the Church's power to be very great, because it hath dispensed with a precept of the Decalogue."[6] In other words, the Roman Catholic Church claimed to have changed the Lord's Day from the seventh day to Sunday!

Fifteen years later the Catholic Council of Trent began

(1545–1563), in order to determine definitively "the doctrines of the Church in answer to the [perceived] heresies of the Protestants; [and to remove] the numerous abuses that had developed in it."[7] In the speech that opened the seventeenth session of the Council of Trent in January 1562, Gaspare del Fosso, the archbishop of Reggio, noted an important Catholic distinction between tradition and Scripture. "He openly declared that tradition stood above Scripture. The authority of the church could therefore not be bound to the authority of the Scriptures, because the church had changed circumcision into baptism, Sabbath into Sunday, not by the command of Christ, but by its own authority. With this, to be sure, the last illusion was destroyed, and it was declared that tradition does not signify iniquity, but continual inspiration."[8] Clearly, the Catholic Church believed its traditions held precedence over the Word of God!

With *sola Scriptura* (Scripture alone) as one of the core tenets of the Reformation, Luther rightly believed in what Scripture teaches and opposed human traditions, even though he did not keep the seventh-day Sabbath. In response to Luther and other Reformers spurning Catholic tradition, Catholic theologian Johann Eck answered that if you "turn from the Church to the Scriptures alone, then you must keep the Sabbath with the Jews, which has been kept from the beginning of the world."[9] Luther's Reformation did not embrace all biblical truths, but it was a step in the right direction.

The papacy changed its approach

While the Catholic Church chided Protestants during the sixteenth-century Reformation for protesting against the Catholic Church when they also kept the Catholic Sunday, the Catholic Church has altered its tactics in modern times.

In the post–Vatican II (1962–1965) era, the Catholic Church is reaching out for the first time to embrace all churches and religions for ecumenical reasons—to unite them and become the leader over them. Now the Catholic Church does not direct attention to its assertion that it changed the Sabbath day. With ecumenism on its agenda, the Catholic Church now focuses on getting the "separated brethren" (Orthodox and Protestant) to return to the fold,[10] and stressing their Sunday-change claim would not help, but hinder, this cause.

Keeping Sunday in honor of the resurrection is not new, for it has a long history among Christians, a history that is used to prove that the Sabbath has been changed. In the face of this attempt to change God's law, the only safe position is a retreat to the clear command of God. "Remember the Sabbath day to keep it holy. Six days you shall labor and do all your work, but the seventh day is the Sabbath of the Lord your God." (Exodus 20:8–10).

------

1. White, *Patriarchs and Prophets*, 37.

2. Ibid., 38.

3. Ellen G. White, *Thoughts From the Mount of Blessing* (Mountain View, CA: Pacific Press® Pub. Assn., 1956), 48.

4. White, *Patriarchs and Prophets*, 41.

5. Herman Bavinck, *Reformed Dogmatics*, vol. 4, *Holy Spirit, Church, and New Creation*, ed. John Bolt (Grand Rapids, MI: Baker, 2008), 252.

6. The Augsburg Confession, art. 28, sec. 33, quoted in Philip Schaff, *The Creeds of Christendom* (Grand Rapids, MI: Baker Books, 1996), 3:64.

7. Johann Peter Kirsch, "Council of Trent," in *The Catholic Encyclopedia*, vol. 15 (New York: Robert Appleton Co., 1912), http://www.newadvent.org/cathen /15030c.htm.

8. Heinrich Julius Holtzmann, *Kanon und Tradition* (Ludwigsburg: Druck and Verlag von Ferd. Riehm, 1859), 263, quoted in Don F. Neufeld and Julia Neuffer, eds., *Seventh-day Adventist Bible Students' Source Book*, vol. 9 (Washington, DC: Review and Herald® Pub. Assn., 1962), 888.

9. Johann Eck, *Enchiridion locorum communium adversus Lutherum et alios hostes ecclesiae* (1533), quoted in Robert L. Odom, *Sunday in Roman Paganism* (Washington, DC: Review and Herald® Pub. Assn., 1944), 246.

10. Second Vatican Council, *Unitatis Redintegratio* (Decree on Ecumenism), Vatican, accessed August 22, 2017, http://www.vatican.va/archive/hist_councils /ii_vatican_council/documents/vat-ii_decree_19641121_unitatis-redintegratio _en.html.

CHAPTER 7

Christ's Teachings to Fit Us for Heaven

In a previous chapter, we noted the terrible suffering Christ endured in Gethsemane, during His trials, and on the cross. But His suffering took place throughout much of His life, for Satan hated Him more than anyone else and worked harder to cause Him to fail than any other person. Satan's future depended on defeating Christ.

"There was never one who walked among men more cruelly slandered than the Son of man. He was derided and mocked because of His unswerving obedience to the principles of God's holy law. They hated Him without a cause. Yet He stood calmly before His enemies, declaring that reproach is a part of the Christian's legacy, counseling His followers how to meet the arrows of malice, bidding them not to faint under persecution."[1] In this chapter, we will look at Christ's teachings and and how they prepare us for life in heaven.

The mount of blessing

"More than fourteen centuries before Jesus,"[2] the preincarnate Christ gave through Moses the curses (Deuteronomy 27:9–26; 28:15–68) and blessings (Deuteronomy 28:1–14) that would come upon Israel if the people disobeyed or obeyed God. If obedient, it was promised that "the LORD your God will set you high above all the nations on earth" (verse 1).

This never happened because Israel failed to obey. But later, while on a mountainside, Christ would give them another set of blessings—the Beatitudes. This Sermon on the Mount was Christ's teaching on how to be fit for heaven (Matthew 5–7). But before we present some of the blessings, it is important to grasp the context and purpose of the blessings.

Although there were some good leaders besides the prophets, many Old Testament leaders led Israel to receive the curses, and Israel's leaders continued to do the same in Christ's day. By His time, they were jealous of the greatest blessing to come to Israel—Christ—and would give Him up to the Romans to be crucified. They were blind to the fact that it was Christ's "mission, by making men partakers of the divine nature, to bring them into harmony with the principles of the law of heaven."[3] "God offered them, in His Son, the perfect righteousness of the law. If they would open their hearts fully to receive Christ, then the very life of God, His love, would dwell in them, transforming them into His own likeness; and thus through God's free gift they would possess the righteousness which the law requires."[4] With this background before us, we can appreciate the blessings Christ had to give His people and to us.

"Blessed are those who mourn, for they will be comforted" *(Matthew 5:4).* Christ speaks about mourning over sin. Looking to Christ hanging on the cross, one sees that "it is sin which scourged and crucified the Lord of glory. He [the sinner] sees that, while he has been loved with unspeakable tenderness, his life has been a continual scene of ingratitude and rebellion. He has forsaken his best Friend and abused heaven's most precious gift. He has crucified to himself the Son of God afresh and pierced anew that bleeding and stricken heart. He is separated from God by a gulf of sin that is broad and black and deep, and he mourns in brokenness of heart."[5] Christ comforts this mourning and sorrow.

Do you need this comfort? Christ longs to give it to you. Think of David as he left Jerusalem when his son Absalom tried to usurp his throne. "David continued up the Mount of

Olives, weeping as he went; his head was covered and he was barefoot" (2 Samuel 15:30). "The Lord was looking pityingly upon him. David was clothed in sackcloth, and his conscience was scourging him. The outward signs of humiliation testified of his contrition. In tearful, heartbroken utterances he presented his case to God, and the Lord did not forsake His servant. Never was David dearer to the heart of Infinite Love than when, conscience-smitten, he fled for his life from his enemies, who had been stirred to rebellion by his own son."[6]

"God would not have us remain pressed down by dumb sorrow, with sore and breaking hearts. He would have us look up and behold His dear face of love. The blessed Saviour stands by many whose eyes are so blinded by tears that they do not discern Him. He longs to clasp our hands, to have us look to Him in simple faith, permitting Him to guide us. His heart is open to our griefs, our sorrows, and our trials. He has loved us with an everlasting love and with loving-kindness compassed us about."[7]

"Blessed are the meek, for they will inherit the earth" (Matthew 5:5). Meekness is not weakness. For example, Scripture says, "The man Moses was very meek, more than all people who were on the face of the earth" (Numbers 12:3, ESV). Moses was not a weak man, but he was meek. "Jesus places meekness among the first qualifications for His kingdom. In His own life and character the divine beauty of this precious grace is revealed."[8] David said that "the meek will inherit the land and enjoy great peace and prosperity" (Psalm 37:11).

"The most precious fruit of sanctification is the grace of meekness. . . . True meekness softens and subdues the heart and gives the mind a fitness for the engrafted word."[9] "Meekness is the inward adorning, which God estimates as of great price. . . . Angels of heaven will register as best adorned those who put on the Lord Jesus Christ and walk with Him in meekness and lowliness of mind."[10]

"Blessed are the merciful, for they will be shown mercy" (Matthew 5:7). "God is Himself the source of all mercy. His name is 'merciful and gracious.' Exodus 34:6. He does not treat us according to our desert. He does not ask if we are worthy of

His love, but He pours upon us the riches of His love, to make us worthy."[11] How merciful is Christ to be willing to suffer for all human guilt in order to save those who accept His free gift! Are we merciful to those who have not shown mercy to us? The indwelling Christ reveals mercy through us, for it is His delight to be merciful.

"Blessed are the pure in heart, for they will see God" (Matthew 5:8). We live in a sin-drenched world. Impurity is all around us, and Satan uses media of every description to drag humanity down to the lowest depths.

What is Christ's definition of purity? What does it involve? You may be surprised that "the words of Jesus, 'Blessed are the pure in heart,' have a deeper meaning—not merely pure in the sense in which the world understands purity, free from that which is sensual, pure from lust, but true in the hidden purposes and motives of the soul, free from pride and self-seeking, humble, unselfish, childlike."[12]

This purity of heart and mind can be found only in Jesus. "Therefore, there is now no condemnation for those who are in Christ Jesus, because through Christ Jesus the law of the Spirit who gives life has set you free from the law of sin and death" (Romans 8:1, 2). Praise God!

Perfection is not performance, but complete *dependence* on Christ who can do for us that which we can never do for ourselves. Without Christ, we have no hope. He died in our place, bearing our guilt; He intercedes in heaven to forgive our sins; and He reigns within us, if we are willing, and gives us victory over sin. As we become fully dependent on Christ, He transforms our hearts and desires. No wonder heaven begins now as we live in and through Him!

Some people delay and say, "I am young. I have all my life before me. There's plenty of time for me to get serious about being saved." But delaying such an important decision isn't wise. Scripture says, "Now is the day of salvation" (2 Corinthians 6:2). Grab the opportunity while you can!

"Blessed are those who are persecuted because of righteousness, for theirs is the kingdom of heaven" (Matthew 5:10). Ponder long this

wonderful truth: "Through trials and persecutions, the glory—character—of God is revealed in His chosen ones. The church of God, hated and persecuted by the world, are educated and disciplined in the school of Christ. They walk in narrow paths on earth; they are purified in the furnace of affliction. They follow Christ through sore conflicts; they endure self-denial and experience bitter disappointments; but their painful experience teaches them the guilt and woe of sin, and they look upon it with abhorrence. Being partakers of Christ's sufferings, they are destined to be partakers of His glory."[13]

Christ's teaching on signs of the end time

We now move away from the mount of blessing, which was earlier in Christ's ministry, to the Mount of Olives (Matthew 24:3), which was near the end of His ministry on Earth. The disciples asked Christ, "What will be the sign of your coming and of the end of the age?" (verse 3). They expected a specific answer; instead, Christ replied, "Watch out that no one deceives you" (verse 4). He uses this word *deceive* four times in Matthew 24. He was concerned that "great signs and wonders" could deceive "even the elect" (verse 24).

The disciples' question asks about "the sign" in the singular. But Christ went on to speak of various signs of the end time. It seemed that He ignored their specific question. He would come to that later, but first He was concerned about the treacherous lies that could rob His followers of eternal life.

Besides the warning about deception, Christ mentioned crises that would occur prior to His coming: wars (verse 6), famines and earthquakes (verse 7), persecutions (verse 9), and many apostasies (verses 10, 12). He also exhorted His followers to keep the Sabbath (verse 20) and to study the abomination mentioned in Daniel (verse 15; see Daniel 9:27; 11:31; 12:11).

Finally, after talking about all these things, Christ answered the question the disciples had asked. He said, "Then will appear *the sign* [singular] of the Son of Man in heaven. And then all the peoples of the earth will mourn when they see the Son of Man coming on the clouds of heaven, with power and great glory" (Matthew 24:30; emphasis added). His glory will flash like lightning across the heavens (verse 27). A counterfeit Christ, out in the desert or in an inner room, cannot come through the heavens with blinding glory (verses 15–26). But a counterfeit Christ will powerfully deceive people and rob them of salvation (verse 24).

Christ will descend from heaven, His people will ascend to meet Him in the air, and together they will go to heaven (1 Thessalonians 4:16, 17). This is *the sign* that Christ urged His followers to know. This sign is more important than all other signs, for this sign in the heavens radically distinguishes the genuine coming of Christ from the counterfeit on earth.

Ellen G. White explains the sign of Christ's return more fully:

> As the crowning act in the great drama of deception, Satan himself will personate Christ. . . .
>
> . . . Satan is not permitted to counterfeit the manner of Christ's advent. . . .
>
> . . . Satan will, if possible, prevent them [the believers] from obtaining a preparation to stand in that day. He will so arrange affairs as to hedge up their way, entangle them with earthly treasures, cause them to carry a heavy, wearisome burden, that their hearts may be overcharged with the cares of this life and the day of trial may come upon them as a thief.[14]

How sad it would be to spend a lifetime carrying unneeded burdens. If you are weighed down with the cares of life, Christ invites you, "Come to me, all you who are weary and burdened, and I will give you rest" (Matthew 11:28).

Christ's parable of the ten virgins

In Christ's parable of the ten virgins, five virgins were wise and five were foolish (Matthew 25:1–13). All of them were virgins; all had lamps; all had some oil in their lamps; all looked forward to the bridegroom's arrival; and all fell asleep. But the foolish virgins had no extra oil like their wise counterparts. That was the crucial difference.

Like the ten virgins, we live in the time when the Bridegroom, Christ, is coming soon. Christ's virgins need the infilling of the latter rain. The foolish virgins have not prepared for the latter rain. They are superficial believers and are not involved in being fitted for heaven and helping others to be ready either. Foolish virgins have "a form of godliness" but deny the power of God available to them (2 Timothy 3:5).

What do the foolish virgins need to learn? The battle for victory is not over sins (or even discovering those things we do wrong without realizing it); rather, it is to become and remain connected with Jesus Christ, who saves us from sin. Then God will supply the victory. "Thanks be to God, who in Christ always leads us in triumph" (2 Corinthians 2:14, RSV).

The foolish virgins were satisfied with so little oil when they could have had so much. What a tragedy! An overflowing fullness of the latter rain is available to believers through a dependent union with Christ; but like the church in Laodicea, foolish people keep Christ knocking at their door and never open it. Christ longs to enter in and pleads with every heart, "Behold, I stand at the door and knock; if anyone hears My voice and opens the door, I will come in to him and will dine with him, and he with Me" (Revelation 3:20).

----

1. White, *Thoughts From the Mount of Blessing*, 32.
2. Ibid., 1.
3. Ibid., 50.
4. Ibid., 54.
5. Ibid., 9.
6. Ibid., 11.
7. Ibid., 12.
8. Ibid., 14.
9. Ellen G. White, *The Sanctified Life* (Washington, DC: Review and Herald® Pub. Assn., 1937), 14.
10. Ibid., 16.
11. White, *Thoughts From the Mount of Blessing*, 22.
12. Ibid., 25.
13. Ibid., 31.
14. White, *The Great Controversy*, 624, 625.

CHAPTER 8

Worship the Creator

Eleven disciples met with the resurrected Christ and worshiped Him (Matthew 28:16, 17). Then Jesus told them: "All authority in heaven and on earth has been given to me. Therefore go and make disciples of all nations, baptizing them in the name of the Father and of the Son and of the Holy Spirit, and teaching them to obey everything I have commanded you. And surely I am with you always, to the very end of the age" (verses 18–20).

This Great Commission at the end of Christ's life on Earth can be compared to the first of the three angels' messages found in Revelation 14:6–12. Given to Christ's disciples as a warning message at the end time of human history, the three angels' messages are an extension of the Great Commission, and they must go to the whole world. Both commissions are the eternal gospel, which is greatly needed by a world that is adrift, without chart or compass.

In the Great Commission, Christ commanded His disciples to teach others everything He taught them, and we have the same mandate in presenting the three angels' messages. These messages must not be softened by the culture of ecumenism (the unification of churches on common doctrines) any more than the first Great Commission needed to be confined by the views of the Jewish culture in the disciples' time.

Ellen White tells us that the three angels' messages "constitute a threefold warning" that are to "prepare the inhabitants of the earth for the Lord's second coming."[1] They caution two kinds of people in particular: those who are Christ's followers in "Babylon the Great" (Revelation 14:8)—believers who are in the apostate churches that have united with the papacy; and those who are opposed to Christ. This warning to the believers in the apostate churches is climaxed in the call of the angel of Revelation 18: " 'Come out of her, my people,' so that you will not share in her sins, so that you will not receive any of her plagues" (verse 4). Those people who are opposed to Christ, who remain in Babylon the Great, are told what punishment they will receive for their rebellion against Christ and His followers. The first group of people reveres God, but the second only fears His judgment.

These messages are not optional. They are absolutely vital in order to prepare God's people for making the decision between the two sides of the cosmic controversy. All humans need to hear these messages so they can make their choice.

Unfolding the first message

Let's look at the first message: "Then I saw another angel flying in midair, and he had the eternal gospel to proclaim to those who live on the earth—to every nation, tribe, language and people. He said in a loud voice, 'Fear God and give him glory, because the hour of his judgment has come. Worship him who made the heavens, the earth, the sea and the springs of water' " (Revelation 14:6, 7). Clearly, the message is part of the eternal gospel and must be taken to the ends of the earth.

"Fear God" (verse 7). What does "Fear God" mean? To fear God means to " 'revere, respect, hold in awe' (Ps. 111:10; Prov. 3:7; 9:10). But it can also mean 'Be afraid' for those who do not take Him seriously (Revelation 6:15–17)."[2] *Reverence* and *fear* indicate the two responses from the two different sides of the cosmic controversy.

Those who believe in Christ and remain in a loving, saving

relationship with Him do not experience the fear that non-believers have: "There is no fear in love. But perfect love drives out fear, because fear has to do with punishment" (1 John 4:18). "For God did not send his Son into the world to condemn the world, but to save the world through him. Whoever believes in him is not condemned, but whoever does not believe stands condemned already because they have not believed in the name of God's one and only Son" (John 3:17, 18). There is no need for genuine Christians to fear the judgment. But those opposed to Christ will fear the judgment that is described in the second and third angels' messages, for it is punishment unmixed with mercy.

"Give him glory" (Revelation 14:7). Those who truly revere God give Him glory. They do not glory in themselves, for they see nothing praiseworthy in themselves. They admit, "All our righteous acts are like filthy rags" (Isaiah 64:6). Even the sinless Savior said, "If I glorify myself, my glory means nothing" (John 8:54). Jesus' reverence for the Father was clear when He said to the Father: "I have brought you glory on earth by finishing the work you gave me to do" (John 17:4). God's end-time saints will bring glory to God through remaining true during persecution, preaching the three angels' messages, and completing the Great Commission.

"The hour of his judgment has come" (Revelation 14:7). Seventh-day Adventists believe this judgment began in October 1844.[3]

[Christ] was inaugurated as our great High Priest and began His intercessory ministry at the time of His ascension. In 1844, at the end of the prophetic period of 2300 days, He entered the second and last phase of His atoning ministry. It is a work of investigative judgment which is part of the ultimate disposition of all sin, typified by the cleansing of the ancient Hebrew sanctuary on the Day of Atonement. In that typical service the sanctuary was cleansed with the blood of animal sacrifices, but the heavenly things are purified with the perfect sacrifice of the blood of Jesus. The investigative judgment reveals to heavenly intelligences who among the dead are asleep in Christ and therefore, in Him, are deemed worthy to have part in the first resurrection. It also makes manifest who among the living are abiding in Christ. . . . This judgment vindicates the justice of God in saving those who believe in Jesus. It declares that those who have remained loyal to God shall receive the kingdom.[4]

When the investigation is complete and Christ is certain that everyone has made their choice, He will return to redeem His children.

Redemption and restoration

Beyond redemption, Christ's ultimate goal in His redemptive work is restoration. Redemption by itself is not enough. For redemption is only fulfilled in the restoration of the universe. This is the time when "sin and sinners are no more"[5] and the controversy is over forever. This involves the cosmic controversy. Whereas Christ's redemptive work is for humans, His restorative work is for all created beings.

What does restoration require? It demands that God is proven to be just, in spite of Satan's lies against God. For this reason, the restoration ministry involves three judgments: (1) the pre-Advent judgment,[6] (2) the millennial judgment, and (3) the postmillennial judgment (Revelation 20:7–15). God doesn't need these judgments, because He is omniscient and thus knows everything (Psalm 33:13–15; 139:1–4; 147:4; Isaiah 46:9, 10; Matthew 10:29, 30; Acts 15:8; Romans 11:33; Ephesians 3:10). "The Lord knows those who are his" (2 Timothy 2:19). Jesus declares, "I know my sheep" (John 10:14). These texts show that God holds these judgments for the benefit of created beings.

The reasons most Christians reject these later judgments is because (1) they believe these judgments demean the judgment at the cross, and (2) they have not fully understood the cosmic controversy and the need for these judgments. They have not grasped the seriousness of Satan's charges against Christ and the need to set the record right so that sin can be eradicated without the possibility of it ever arising again. In other words, if the fullest revelation of Satan's rebellion is not exposed, then a lingering question of God's justice would keep the universe from being restored to its precontroversy status.

Focus in these judgments

The focus of the pre-Advent judgment is clearly delineated in Daniel 7. The two sides of the cosmic controversy are in this judgment: the papacy (the little horn) and God's people. The papacy is presented as boastful (verses 8, 11, 20) and is opposed to God and to God's people (verses 24, 25).

"But the court will sit, and his [the papacy's] power will be taken away and completely destroyed forever" (verse 26). Daniel said, "I kept looking until the beast [the papacy] was slain and its body destroyed and thrown into the blazing fire" (verse 11b).

What about God's people? Their focus is crucial. They focus their attention on Christ and His sacrifice. At Calvary, Christ died to redeem lost humanity and to destroy sin. On the basis of Calvary, He now intercedes and judges. Those who cling to the Cross receive deliverance, and those who refuse the Cross choose to be destroyed. It is the reception or rejection of Calvary that determines human destiny. This is the essence of the pre-Advent judgment. This is why there is no fear in this judgment for Christ's followers—there is only great rejoicing!

Do you fear the coming judgment? Some do, but there is no need to fear if you remain in a relationship of love with the Judge. Remember it is the Crucified One who is in charge of the judgment. During the adjudication process, He is still interceding for those who depend on Him and love Him. Let Christ wrap His mighty arms of love around you and hold you close. It's worth repeating—His perfect love casts out fear (see 1 John 4:18).

Worshiping the Creator

"Worship him who made the heavens, the earth, the sea and the springs of water" (Revelation 14:7). The first angel calls us to worship God, but evolution has become a religion of sorts for many. In fact, Darwinian evolution was beginning to plague the planet at the time the pre-Advent judgment began.[7]

When evolutionary changes—from molecule to man—are assumed as factual across the stretch of deep time, we are confronted with speculation, not scientific fact. What we have in evolution is a human theory that cannot be verified. Evolution is a dictatorial view that discounts the supernatural and serves no more effectively in the world of ideas than a dictator does in the world of diplomacy.

When God, or the supernatural, is removed from the realm of causality, something has to fill the vacuum. Not only has naturalism taken the place of God, but evolution has become a "religion" in the place of biblical religion that worships the Creator. Physicist H. S. Lipson observes that "evolution became in a sense a scientific religion; almost all scientists have accepted it and many are prepared to 'bend' their observations to fit in with it."[8] Alvin Plantinga noted that "evolution has deep religious connections; deep connections with how we understand ourselves at the most fundamental level."[9]

What is the bottom line of evolutionary theory? Humans are an unplanned accident, and their lives are as self-centered and purposeless as the process. They have no more value than the alleged process that brought them onto the planet. Their future has no goal any more than their past. They are surrounded by continuing chance.

If this is true, then why is it that humans search for meaning and purpose and have a desire to worship? These innate yearnings are universally shared by all races, cultures, and ages. They witness to the time when humans were made in the image of God and were capable of communion with God (Genesis 1:26, 27; 2:1–3, 7). They indicate that though sin has damaged the image of God within, sin has not destroyed this image.

Christ's followers are called to worship God as Creator. The greatest evidence of Creation was not in Eden but in Bethlehem. When Jesus was born of Mary through the power of the Holy Spirit, we see a creative act of God in history (Matthew 1:20). He created in Eden and in the Incarnation. Both were equally supernatural and both had a purpose; neither was confined to the chance of naturalism. It is reassuring to know that chance has never been part of God's plan for creation or redemption.

The second and third angels' messages

Having established God as Creator, the second angel's message goes on to point out the fall of Babylon the Great (Revelation 14:8). Babylon, which is often referred to as a woman, is fallen because she induced all nations to unite with her instead of her being united with Christ. Spiritual adultery is what this is. Babylon the Great is just as much a counterfeit religion as evolution—both replace Christ with human ideas and plans.

The third angel warns, " 'If anyone worships the beast [the papacy] and its image [a persecuting union of church and state, like the papacy] and receives its mark [Sunday] on their forehead or on the hand, they, too, will drink the wine of God's fury.' . . . This calls for patient endurance on the part of the people of God who keep his commands and remain faithful to Jesus" (verses 9, 10, 12). The third angel's message refers to God's judgments that Babylon the Great will receive in the end time (Revelation 16–18). God's fury is without mercy, for Babylon's counterfeit religion will be global and will cause the civil powers to enforce their Sunday-observance law by a death decree (Revelation 13:1–15). This is the ultimate global replacement of Christ.

This counterfeit religion demands the rejection of the seventh-day Sabbath that was chosen by the Creator as a memorial of His creation for all humans (cf. Genesis 2:1–3; Mark 2:27, 28).[10] In its place, Sunday is substituted for the true Sabbath, just as the pope usurps Christ as the head of the church and exalts himself as God in place of the only true God (2 Thessalonians 2:3, 4). In the end time, people will worship "the dragon [Satan; see Revelation 12:9]" because he has given "authority to the beast [the papacy]," and they will also worship "the beast" (Revelation 13:4; cf. verses 8, 12).

But there is no need to fear these end-time events. Christ has defeated the enemy and delivered His people. In the Cross, there is great rejoicing!

---

1. White, *The Great Controversy*, 435.

2. *Andrews Study Bible*, note on Revelation 14:7.

3. Seventh-day Adventists believe that the 2,300 prophetic days mentioned in Daniel 8:14 ended in 1844. It is at this point that Christ began the work of the investigative judgment—the cleansing of the sanctuary. For more information, see the *Andrews Study Bible*, note on Daniel 8:14. See also White, *The Great Controversy*, 479, 480, 486.

4. General Conference of Seventh-day Adventists, *Seventh-day Adventists Believe*, 347, 348.

5. White, *The Great Controversy*, 678.

6. The present judgment is called *pre-Advent*, denoting its time, and *investigative*, denoting its method (Revelation 14:6, 7). It has been in session since October 22, 1844, and will continue until the close of human probation.

7. Charles Darwin's *On the Origin of Species* was already largely written by 1844, even though it was not published until 1859.

8. H. S. Lipson, "A Physicist Looks at Evolution," *Physics Bulletin* 31, no. 4 (1980): 138.

9. Alvin Plantinga, "When Faith and Reason Clash: Evolution and the Bible," *Christian Scholar's Review* 21, no. 1 (September 1991): 17.

10. See also White, *The Great Controversy*, 437.

End-Time Deceptions

In His teaching on the earth's final events, Christ admonished His disciples, "Watch out that no one deceives you" (Matthew 24:4). He warned them that many will be deceived, and if possible, even the elect (verses 5, 11, 24).

False union of Christians

The misuse of Christ's prayer in John 17 has contributed to a powerful end-time deception. Christ said, "My prayer is not for them alone. I pray also for those who will believe in me through their message, that all of them may be one, Father, just as you are in me and I am in you. May they also be in us so that the world may believe that you have sent me" (John 17:20, 21). For many Christians, this prayer is interpreted as indicating that the unification of churches (called *ecumenism*) is Christ's will. Through this union, they believe, the world will be convinced of Christ's witness and the gospel. But Christ's prayer on unity is often not read in its full context. Believers are to be joined together in the truth: "Sanctify them by the truth; your word is truth" (verse 17). True unity is based upon truth—God's Word—and nothing less.

The union of all churches is thought to be the only way to defeat secularism—a common enemy of Christian churches.

But ecumenical leaders do not realize that a union based on nontruths is itself a kind of secularism. Ecumenical agreement on common beliefs at the expense of unique articles of faith rejects truths from God's Word.

Five hundred years ago, the Protestant Reformation was all about truth. At first, the Magisterial Reformers, such as Luther, Calvin, and Zwingli, did not want to break away from the Catholic Church. They wanted to see corruptions removed from the church's systems. But they evaluated the medieval church by Scripture and clearly saw that it was teaching anti-Christian ideas—teachings opposed to Christ and biblical truths.

What would those giants of the Reformation think of modern Protestantism's retreat from the Bible as the rule of faith and practice? They would be dismayed and urge every sincere Christian to examine their faith and be wary of man-made doctrines posing as spiritual enlightenment.

False prophets

Christ warned His followers that false prophets would try to deceive them (Matthew 24:24). And over the centuries false teachings began to creep into the faith. These teachings, taken from old and new traditions, claimed that the Bible is an incomplete revelation, and new ideas, running counter to biblical truth, were accepted as divine revelation. For example, consider these teachings about Mary:

- 1854: Pope Pius IX issued the dogma on the immaculate conception of Mary.[1]
- 1896: Pope Leo XIII issued the dogma that Mary was the "Mediatrix to the Mediator."[2] *Mediatrix* means Mary gave the Redeemer, the Source of all graces, to the world. In this way, she is the channel of all graces.
- 1904: Pope Pius X issued the dogma that Mary is the restorer of the fallen world and the dispenser of all the grace Jesus won for us by His death.[3]
- 1918: Pope Benedict XV said Mary redeemed the

human race in cooperation with Christ.[4]

- 1943: Pope Pius XII issued the encyclical *Mystici corporis Christi*, which states that it was Mary who offered her Son on Golgotha to the eternal Father, and it was through her prayers that the Holy Spirit was poured out upon the church at Pentecost.[5]
- 1950: Pope Pius XII also issued the dogma of the bodily assumption of Mary to heaven. Because she was without sin, she was taken immediately to heaven after her life on Earth.[6]

These human traditions are claimed to be divine revelation, and the Catholic Church requires that they be believed as such. In particular, these ideas about Mary are based on Satan's lie that humans are immortal (Genesis 3:4) and go on to allege that Mary now lives in heaven.

The Roman Church promotes Satan's view on immortality as do modern Protestant churches. However, natural immortality is a pagan idea.[7] We have been warned of this: "Through the two great errors, the immortality of the soul and Sunday sacredness, Satan will bring the people under his deceptions."[8]

In the First Vatican Council (1870), the popes were declared to be infallible and thus could not make a mistake when speaking on doctrine from their chair. This belief places them above Scripture and does not allow Scripture to be its own final interpreter. Doesn't papal infallibility question biblical authority? Present Protestant leaders hardly whisper against the false teachings about Mary mentioned above. They no longer protest. They lack the discernment of the early Reformers and are inching closer to an ecumenical union that is not based on truth.

In contrast to these present-day leaders, listen to the great Martin Luther. He was fearless and stood for the right, whatever the consequences. Luther wrote,

The pope is a god on earth over everything heavenly, earthly, spiritual, and secular, and all is his own. No one is permitted to say to him: "What are you doing?" That is the abomination and stench of which Christ speaks in Matt. 24 [:15] "So when you see the desolating sacrilege spoken of by the prophet Daniel [Dan. 9:27; 12:11], standing in the holy place (let the reader understand)," etc. And St Paul writes: "He will take his seat in the temple of God (that is, in Christendom), proclaiming himself to be God" [Cf. 2 Thess. 2:4].[9]

This reminds me of Ellen White's stirring statement that was displayed on the wall behind the pulpit in the men's chapel in Newbold College in England: "The greatest want of the world is the want of men—men who will not be bought or sold, men who in their inmost souls are true and honest, men who do not fear to call sin by its right name, men whose conscience is as true to duty as the needle to the pole, men who will stand for the right though the heavens fall."[10]

Protestant ecumenical leaders have joined Catholic leaders in using historical-critical methods (placing human ideas above God's revelation) in interpreting Scripture, abandoning the Reformation principle of *sola Scriptura*—using the Bible to interpret itself. In fact, Scripture is no longer considered revelation by many Protestant scholars; it is considered only a witness to the revelations received by the biblical writers; a human response to revelation rather than divine revelation itself.

Of course, Scripture is not a common book. Peter makes that clear. "For prophecy never had its origin in the human will, but prophets, though human, spoke from God as they were carried along by the Holy Spirit" (2 Peter 1:21).

The Reformation, and its emphasis on the Bible, was an inconvenient challenge for the medieval church, and action was taken at the Council of Trent (1545–1563) to launch the Counter-Reformation. This movement sought to destroy Protestantism by introducing futurism (fulfillment of prophecy in the distant future) to replace the Reformers' historicist reading of prophecy (a natural unfolding of events in past, present, and future history).

Despite these efforts, the Reformation survived and flourished. And yet it seems that modern protestants have forgotten that Bibles were once banned and burned. The Council of Trent claimed that tradition was equal with the Bible (1546), and the Second Vatican Council (1962–1965) declared divine revelation and human traditions are to be equally venerated.[11] How could contemporary Protestant leaders forget these things?

This is a blatant change of God's holy Word that warrants Revelation's caution. "I warn everyone who hears the words of the prophecy of this scroll [Revelation]: If anyone adds anything to them, God will add to that person the plagues described in this scroll. And if anyone takes words away from this scroll of prophecy, God will take away from that person any share in the tree of life and in the Holy City, which are described in this scroll" (Revelation 22:18, 19).

Sunday worship

We now come to another false teaching of the papacy. It plays a major role in earth's final events. The Sunday issue will deceive nearly the whole world (Revelation 13:1–4).

Sunday worship traces its origins back to the sun worship practiced in pagan Rome. Later, the early Christian church gradually replaced Christ's seventh-day Sabbath with Rome's pagan Sunday. There was a time, as we saw in chapter 6, when the papacy boasted that this change of the Sabbath day proved that the Catholic Church's authority was greater than God's authority.

Most Christians today view Sunday as the new Sabbath in honor of Christ's resurrection. These believers, many of them sincere, overlook the fact that the day before Christ's resurrection—on the seventh-day Sabbath—He rested in the grave, and His followers honored the Sabbath also (Luke 23:56; 24:1–6). They miss Christ's teaching concerning keeping the Sabbath in A.D. 70, when pagan Rome would attack Jerusalem. Jesus warned them: "Pray that your flight will not take place in winter or on the Sabbath" (Matthew 24:20).

The greatest end-time deception

Mariolatry and Sunday worship are examples of false teachings, but maybe the most sinister deception of all is the original lie that was spun in Eden, "You shall not surely die" (Genesis 3:4). It is in this context that Satan used his trump card—seeing is believing. Sadly, Eve fell for the clever ruse. "When the woman saw that the fruit of the tree was good for food and pleasing to the eye, and also desirable for gaining wisdom, she took some and ate it" (Genesis 3:6). In the end time, Satan will pull all the stops and stage one final grand delusion.

> As the crowning act in the great drama of deception, Satan himself will personate Christ. The church has long professed to look to the Saviour's advent as the consummation of her hopes. Now the great deceiver will make it appear that Christ has come. In different parts of the earth, Satan will manifest himself among men as a majestic being of dazzling brightness, resembling the description of the Son of God given by John in the Revelation. Revelation 1:13-15. The glory that surrounds him is unsurpassed by anything that mortal eyes have yet beheld. The shout of triumph rings out upon the air: "Christ has come! Christ has come!"[12]

You can imagine how television stations around the world will herald the alleged coming of Christ as the greatest news event ever. Long will persons stay glued to their televisions and watch everything the assumed Christ does, what He teaches, and where He is seen next. In keen anticipation, they will long to see him come to a place near where they live. They will throng to see him personally. This will be the stuff of history: never before will a glorious event like this have occurred. The people will not want to miss it for anything. Excitement will fill the airwaves and rivet the attention of billions.

Living in the end time will be hard, with its many wars, natural disasters, strife, and envy. People will fear for their lives, and they will fear what is coming in the future. But the alleged coming of Christ will change all this. Hope will replace hopelessness. What a transformation! It will be party time again! There will be only one topic that absorbs the masses: "What a time to be alive!" "He's coming to our city this weekend." "Let's go out and take it all in." "Let's celebrate!"

At various times and places, the people will "prostrate themselves in adoration before him [the assumed Christ], while he lifts up his hands and pronounces a blessing upon them, as Christ blessed His disciples when He was upon the earth. His voice" will be "soft and subdued, yet full of melody. In gentle, compassionate tones" he will present "some of the same gracious, heavenly truths which the Saviour uttered"; he will heal "the diseases of the people."[13]

"What a weekend that was! I was healed," one will say joyously. "I didn't have money for a doctor, but Christ touched me, and I felt his healing power. Praise his name!"

"Oh, his voice was so beautiful," another will chime in.

"I loved the truths he taught," a third jubilant person will add. "This weekend will never be forgotten."

The world will watch the assumed Christ speak. He will claim to have changed the Sabbath to Sunday; he will bless Sunday and command that all humanity keep Sunday holy. He will declare "that those who persist in keeping holy the seventh day are blaspheming his name by refusing to listen to his angels sent to them with light and truth. This is the strong, almost overmastering delusion."[14] Undoubtedly, many will fall for this false Christ.

But why will they be deceived? Scripture says they will accept the deception because they have embraced a form of godliness but not the power of the gospel. "There will be terrible times in the last days. People will be lovers of themselves, lovers of money, boastful, proud, abusive, disobedient to their parents, ungrateful, unholy, without love, unforgiving, slanderous, without self-control, brutal, not lovers of the good, treacherous, rash, conceited, lovers of pleasure rather than lovers of God—having a form of godliness but denying its power. Have nothing to do with such people" (2 Timothy 3:1–5).

Preparation for the End Time

The apostate church, false prophets, false Christs, and Satan's impersonation of Christ are all forms of godliness, but all are end-time deceptions. Each one operates under a veneer that makes them look good while masking their deadly errors. Christ spoke of people like this: "On the outside you appear to people as righteous but on the inside you are full of hypocrisy and wickedness" (Matthew 23:28).

Will Satan have full control?

"God never forces the will or the conscience; but Satan's constant resort—to gain control of those whom he cannot otherwise seduce—is compulsion by cruelty."[15] "As the defenders of truth refuse to honor the Sunday-sabbath, some of them will be thrust into prison, some will be exiled, some will be treated as slaves. To human wisdom all this now seems impossible; but as the restraining Spirit of God shall be withdrawn from men, and they shall be under the control of Satan, who hates the divine precepts, there will be strange developments. The heart can be very cruel when God's fear and love are removed."[16]

But God promises, "Never will I leave you; never will I forsake you" (Hebrews 13:5; cf. Matthew 28:20). "One who sees their every weakness, who is acquainted with every trial, is above all earthly powers; and angels will come to them in lonely cells, bringing light and peace from heaven. The prison will be as a palace; for the rich in faith dwell there, and the gloomy walls will be lighted up with heavenly light."[17]

Christ is in control, and soon after these events He will deliver His followers. What a moment that will be when the saved are ushered into their eternal home. "With unutterable love," Jesus will welcome "His faithful ones to the joy of their Lord."[18]

---

1. Pope Pius IX, *Ineffabilis Deus* (The Immaculate Conception), Papal Encyclicals Online, accessed August 30, 2017, http://www.papalencyclicals.net/pius09 /p9ineff.htm.

2. Pope Leo XIII, *Fidentem Piumquie Animum*, Vatican, accessed August 30, 2017, http://w2.vatican.va/content/leo-xiii/en/encyclicals/documents/hf_l-xiii_enc _20091896_fidentem-piumque-animum.html.

3. Pope Pius X, *Ad Diem Illum Laetissimum* (On the Immaculate Conception), Papal Encyclicals Online, accessed August 30, 2017, http://www.papalencyclicals.net/pius10/p10imcon.htm.

4. Pope Benedict XV, "*Inter Sodalicia*, March 22, 1918," *Acta Apostolicae Sedis* 10 (1918): 182.

5. Pope Pius XII, *Mystici Corporis Christi* (The Mystical Body of Christ, the Church), Vatican, accessed August 30, 2017, http://w2.vatican.va/content/pius-xii /en/encyclicals/documents/hf_p-xii_enc_29061943_mystici-corporis-christi.html.

6. Pope Pius XII, *Munificentissimus Deus* (Defining the Dogma of the Assumption), Papal Encyclicals Online, accessed August 30, 2017, http://www .papalencyclicals.net/pius12/p12munif.htm.

7. White, *The Great Controversy*, 551.

8. Ibid., 588.

9. Martin Luther, *Luther's Works*, vol. 31, *Career of the Reformer 1*, ed. Harold J. Grimm (Philadelphia, PA: Fortress Press, 1957), 393.

10. Ellen G. White, *Education* (Mountain View, CA: Pacific Press® Pub. Assn., 1903), 57.

11. Vatican Council, *The Documents of Vatican II*, ed. Walter M. Abbott (New York: Guild Press, 1966), 117, 2.2.9.

12. White, *The Great Controversy*, 624.

13. Ibid.

14. Ibid.

15. Ibid., 591.

16. Ibid., 608.

17. Ibid., 627.

18. Ibid., 647.

CHAPTER

Spiritualism's Global Triumph

We live in a confused world where a cacophony of voices fills the air. With great angst, people throw absolutes to the wind and wander aimlessly without a compass. Is there a way out of this situation? There is. The cosmic controversy offers hope. It uncovers what is going on in the universe: a battle over truth is underway—God's truth versus Satan's lies.

A crisis of worship

In unmistakable terms, Revelation 14 declares that the looming showdown between God and Satan is all about worship. Three angels loudly proclaim the everlasting gospel to every nation, tribe, and tongue (verses 6–12), calling them to worship the God of creation and the God of redemption.

In a jealous rage, Satan deploys three impure spirits (Revelation 16:13–16) to deceive the people God is seeking to save. Ellen White explains, "Little by little he [Satan] has prepared the way for his masterpiece of deception in the development of spiritualism. He has not yet reached the full accomplishment of his designs; but it will be reached in the last remnant of time. Says the prophet: 'I saw three unclean spirits like frogs; . . . they are the spirits of devils, working miracles, which go forth unto the kings of the earth and of the whole world, to gather them to the battle of that great day of God Almighty.' Revelation 16:13, 14."[1]

This crisis of worship is highlighted again by the fourth angel's message of Revelation 18:

> After this I saw another angel coming down from heaven. He had great authority, and the earth was illuminated by his splendor. With a mighty voice he shouted:
>
> "Fallen! Fallen is Babylon the Great!
> She has become a home for demons
> and a haunt for every evil spirit" (verses 1, 2).

All is not lost, however, because the dire warning goes on to remind us that God has not abandoned those who fellowship in the Roman Church or in apostate Protestant churches. In mercy, He calls out to each one,

> " 'Come out of her, my people,'
> so that you will not share in her sins,
> so that you will not receive any of her plagues;
> for her sins are piled up to heaven" (verses 4, 5).

Deception in Eden

Since the inception of sin, Satan has determined to divert attention from God and direct it to himself. He wants God's throne. He longs for the worship, glory, and adulation only God deserves. In the Garden of Eden, beautifully framed in the tree of the knowledge of good and evil, he planted seeds of uncertainty in Eve's mind. He invited her to distrust God's word. He said she wouldn't die; and most sinister of all, he caused her to trust her senses above all else, even the word of God.

The archdeceiver knew that the key to gaining the worship of the world was in discrediting the clear word of God, and so he bent his energies in that direction. The passing millennia have refined his deceptions, and the modern manifestations are truly frightening.

For example, Vatican II promoted a global-mission program to increase the ranks of the papal church. But the unsettling means of achieving this growth was through the promotion of contemplative traditions and mysticism. A Vatican II decree states, "Working to plant the Church, and thoroughly enriched with the treasures of mysticism adorning the Church's religious tradition, religious communities should strive to give expression to these treasures and to hand them on in a manner harmonious with the nature and the genius of each nation. Let them reflect attentively on how Christian religious life may be able to assimilate the ascetic and contemplative traditions whose seeds were sometimes already planted by God in ancient cultures prior to the preaching of the gospel."[2]

Church growth is a laudable goal but only when energized by unswerving allegiance to the Bible and the gospel of Jesus Christ. Appeals to tradition and mysticism are hardly the stuff of authentic revival and reformation. Yet the same council went on to say that "religious communities of the contemplative and of the active life have so far played, and still do play, a very great role in the evangelization of the world."[3]

These statements from Vatican II constitute the Roman Church's great commission for bringing the world into its embrace. At first blush, it seems harsh to call a church's growth plan spiritual deception and even more extreme to dub it spiritualism, but a closer look shows that the modern masquerade is just as clever as it was in Eden.

The great compromise

In 2017, the world celebrated the five hundredth anniversary of the Protestant Reformation. For five hundred years, politics, religion, and entire nations have been shaped by the Wittenberg monk who championed the Bible as the benchmark of faith and practice. But wouldn't Martin Luther be dismayed if he could see how this great Reformation has been replaced by a great compromise?

Slowly but surely, commitment to sound doctrine is being exchanged for unity at all costs. Pious pragmatism has caused the ecumenical movement to jettison sound doctrine for a platform pleasing to the papacy and Protestantism. Not surprisingly, there is little resistance from within or without the church because our culture does not favor absolutes. This climate of permissiveness is fertile ground for Satan's ensuing deceptions, and his plan is working to perfection. Churches and societies have cut their moorings with Scripture, and the great compromise is shaping up, just as Satan planned.

The emerging church

In this regard, history shows that Catholicism has routinely placed church tradition above Scripture, and a related but distinct deception is the ascendancy of the emerging, or emergent, church. Theologian Stanley Grenz was an early influence in the movement and was noted for placing the community above Scripture. He shifted the focus from doctrines to spirituality.[4] This feature of the emerging church can open the door to spiritual practices that are hazardous to Christianity.

This danger took root during the Middle Ages when pagan influences caused spiritual leaders to leave God's Word and turn to mysticism. Notable influences in this direction were Saint Francis of Assisi and Ignatius of Loyola, who founded the Jesuit order. Their incorporation of mysticism into Christian spirituality laid the foundation for the modern emphasis on experience over doctrine.

Brian D. McLaren, an emerging church leader, has observed that some in the contemplative tradition of Catholicism emphasize how "God may be mystically experienced through contemplation, through a quiet mindfulness."[5] His contemporary Leonard Sweet notes that "people long for the mystery and mysticism of an encounter with God and expect the church to help them get in touch with their experiences."[6] "People want to experience the 'Beyond' in the 'Within.' "[7]

Whether they realize it or not, these emerging-church leaders reject the Holy Spirit by refusing His inspired and holy Word.

Giving primacy to the voice within, they cut themselves off from the divine protection and guidance of the Bible. In this environment, they are more easily deceived by a counterfeit spirit and mistake that encounter as an experience with God. Their earnest desire to understand God is commendable, but they have strayed from the safety of Scripture. "The Spirit clearly says that in later times some will abandon the faith and follow deceiving spirits and things taught by demons" (1 Timothy 4:1).

Jesus promised that the Holy Spirit will guide believers into all truth (see John 16:12–14). Jesus speaks to every sincere seeker through His Word, and the Spirit guides this spiritual experience. But Jesus never speaks contrary to His Word and never in contradiction to His revealed will.

John cautions Christians of all ages with this counsel, "Dear friends, do not believe every spirit, but test the spirits to see whether they are from God, because many false prophets have gone out into the world. This is how you can recognize the Spirit of God: Every spirit that acknowledges that Jesus Christ has come in the flesh is from God, but every spirit that does not acknowledge Jesus is not from God" (1 John 4:1–3).

Be careful of any teaching or experience that does not bring glory to Jesus and that does not harmonize with the Bible. Paul predicted that "the time will come when they will not endure sound doctrine, but according to their own desires, because they have itching ears, they will heap up for themselves teachers; and they will turn their ears away from the truth, and be turned aside to fables" (2 Timothy 4:3, 4, NKJV).

Culture must be subordinate to biblical revelation

God sent biblical revelation to enlighten this fallen world, but Satan uses our culture to neutralize that revelation. In a quest for relevance, modern church movements are seeking to accommodate society, but these movements overlook the fact that mainline churches in America have lost members by embracing "modernist principles in quest of greater relevance."[8]

Humanly speaking, it makes sense that reflecting our culture would increase relevance, but any accommodation of a worldview that is inconsistent with Scripture can only mean trouble. The emerging church—or any movement—that allows a cultural worldview to be its guide is on a dangerous path.

The end point for this approach is a focus on an earthly kingdom.[9] In ancient Israel, God established a theocracy to build His kingdom on earth. He called Abraham out of Ur; and through his descendants, He blessed the world (Genesis 12:1–3). However, it is important to note that the status of this kingdom was conditional (Deuteronomy 28). The sad history of God's chosen people shows that they ultimately went their own way, abandoned God entirely, and rejected His Son by sending Him to die on the cross. This chapter was the final point in God's plan for an earthly kingdom.

In a statement all but ignored by today's kingdom builders, Christ said to Pilate, "My kingdom is not of this world. If it were, my servants would fight to prevent my arrest by the Jewish leaders" (John 18:36). The emerging church, the ecumenical movement, and spiritualism are concerned with an earthly kingdom, proving they misunderstand Christ's words to Pilate. And lest we be smug, even the disciples missed this cue when they gathered around the postresurrection Jesus and asked, "Lord, are you at this time going to restore the kingdom to Israel?" (Acts 1:6). They still didn't get it. They failed to realize that they stood on the threshold of a kingdom built in hearts—a spiritual kingdom of believers called the body of Christ.

The final challenge

Just as the serpent caused Eve to trust her senses more than God's Word, so spiritualism tempts people to trust in supernatural phenomena that run counter to His revealed will. Fallen spirits perform miracles. They teach forcefully, as if bringing new messages from heaven, but their words are dangerous. Our only safety is in the Word of God.

> The people of God are directed to the Scriptures as their safeguard against the influence of false teachers and the delusive power of spirits of darkness. Satan

employs every possible device to prevent men from obtaining a knowledge of the Bible; for its plain utterances reveal his deceptions. . . .

. . . None but those who have fortified the mind with the truths of the Bible will stand through the last great conflict. To every soul will come the searching test: Shall I obey God rather than men? The decisive hour is even now at hand. Are our feet planted on the rock of God's immutable word? Are we prepared to stand firm in defense of the commandments of God and the faith of Jesus?[10]

Of course, it is easy to stand firm when culture and society affirm your position. But it's not so easy when your faith is challenged. The occult, witchcraft, and other spiritualistic manifestations are sweeping the world, preparing the masses for delusion. The majority will no longer smile on Seventh-day Adventists. Allegiance to the Bible will no longer be popular. What then? How will the church fare when it is singled out for scorn and censure?

This scenario is one that believers have long expected; now, while freedom lingers, is the perfect moment to remember the experience of Abraham. Called out of ancient Babylonia, he was willing to be unique for God. He could hardly predict how God would use him to bless the nations of the world, but that did not stop him from moving out in faith. God called and he followed.

Seventh-day Adventists find themselves in a similar situation. The seventh-day Sabbath, the state of the dead, the heavenly sanctuary ministry of Christ, the pre-Advent judgement, and the Second Coming are unique truths the world needs, and following the call to live and preach them is a call to be unique—not popular, but unique. Those heeding this call and following in Abraham's footsteps will be empowered by the Holy Spirit to witness for their faith.

Unfortunately, it is true that not all professed Christians are brothers and sisters in Christ. Jesus made this clear when He warned that the wheat and the tares will grow together until the harvest, and then they will be separated by God (Matthew 13:24–30). It is reasonable to think that the remnant should concern themselves with sharing Jesus and not with sorting out those they deem unbelievers. While it is tempting to pluck the tares from the wheat, that is not the church's job. God alone is judge. He alone possesses infinite love and wisdom. He alone calls out to each heart.

Seventh-day Adventists live in an exciting moment. Blessed beyond all measure, the church is called to share the truth about Jesus via an end-time message that is circling the globe. Many will reject that message, but that is not our concern. We are called to witness, not to manage the results.

Given the sobering nature of this commission, it's worth remembering these words of caution from the pen of inspiration: "The line of distinction between professed Christians and the ungodly is now hardly distinguishable. Church members love what the world loves and are ready to join with them, and Satan determines to unite them in one body and thus strengthen his cause by sweeping all into the ranks of spiritualism."[11]

We do not live in the Garden of Eden today, and people do not gaze at a serpent in a tree. But make no mistake, the issues are unchanged. They swirl around one crucial choice: whether we believe a lie or believe God. In the waning moments of Earth's history, the enemy has conditioned the entire world for deception. Everyone has a choice to make, and right now is the perfect moment to choose Jesus, trust His Word, and share your faith.

---

1. White, *The Great Controversy*, 561.

2. Vatican Council, *The Documents of Vatican II*, 606, 607.

3. Ibid., 627.

4. Stanley J. Grenz, *Revisioning Evangelical Theology: A Fresh Agenda for the 21st Century* (Downers Grove, IL: InterVarsity Press, 1993), 56, 57, 119–122.

5. Brian D. McLaren, *A Generous Orthodoxy* (El Cajon, CA: Youth Specialties Books, 2004), 55.

6. Leonard I. Sweet, *Soul Tsunami: Sink or Swim in New Millennium Culture* (Grand Rapids, MI: Zondervan, 1999), 208.

7. Ibid., 420.

8. Phil Johnson, "Joyriding on the Downgrade at Breakneck Speed: The Dark Side of Diversity," in *Reforming or Conforming? Post-Conservative Evangelicals and the Emerging Church*, eds. Gary L. W. Johnson and Ronald N. Gleason (Wheaton IL: Crossway Books, 2008), 222.

9. For example, see Brian D. McLaren, *The Secret Message of Jesus: Uncovering the Truth That Could Change Everything* (Nashville, TN: Thomas Nelson, 2006), 203, 212.

10. White, *The Great Controversy*, 593, 594.

11. Ibid., 588.

CHAPTER 11

False Worship

After the Flood, the builders of the Tower of Babel set out to "make a name for" themselves (Genesis 11:4). They proudly believed that a structure reaching "to the heavens" would save them (verse 4). Why worry about a global flood when you can save yourself with the work of your own hands? Not only did they disbelieve God's promise to never send another flood (Genesis 9:11–17), they also set a dangerous precedent that would prove the ruin of future generations—salvation by works. This is the premise that lies at the heart of every false religion.

Nothing has changed

Exhibit A in this regard is the Roman Church. Historically, it has been authoritarian in theology and practice from the beginning. However, in the early 1960s, the Vatican II council signified a departure from this attitude toward non-Catholic churches and religions. Pope John XXIII envisioned a more pastoral approach to world evangelism and wanted his church portrayed as the "loving mother of all."[1] But the course correction was a change in tactics rather than a change in theology and church governance.

Terms such as the *Mother Church* and *Mother Mary*

softened the image of the Roman Church, and it was hoped they would serve to woo all churches and religions into its fold. And today the ecumenical movement is proof that there may have been some wisdom in this approach. Nevertheless, the teachings and doctrines of the Catholic Church have remained steadfastly the same. Indeed, the last fifty years have seen Protestants slowly acquiescing to the Roman agenda, steadily joining in with the fall of Babylon the Great (Revelation 14:8–11).

In brief, here are few of the errant teachings reaffirmed by Vatican II:

- Christ handed over the church to Peter.[2]
- The priest of the church continually offers Christ up to God in the Eucharist.[3]
- The pope is "the visible Head of the whole Church."[4]
- Bishops preside "in the place of God."[5]
- The church is the "universal sacrament of salvation."[6]
- Mary "far surpasses all other creatures, both in heaven and on earth."[7]
- Mary is the "Church's model."[8]
- Followers of Christ "raise their eyes to Mary," so "the Church with reverence enters more intimately into the supreme mystery of the Incarnation and becomes ever increasingly like her Spouse."[9]

All of these beliefs are clearly church-centered rather than Christ-centered doctrines. The papal system brings attention and glory to itself, but the true work of the Holy Spirit brings glory to Christ (John 16:14).

At this point in the discussion, there is an important quali-fication to make. In no way does a frank review of these teach-ings cast any aspersions on the wonderful Christians in the Roman Catholic Church. There are many believers in this community of faith who are dedicated to following Jesus and listening to His voice. In eternity, we will enjoy their fellow-ship. I have Catholic friends who are genuine Christians; they love God, worship Him, and study His Word. They are the salt of the earth, and God loves them. So let there be no misunderstanding; starting from a biblical perspective, the focus of our study is the Roman system of faith and teaching. There is no room for personal bias against the members who call themselves Catholic.

Now to a question that needs to be asked: How did we get here? How did the Catholic Church come to consider itself the last word on Christianity? The answer goes all the way back to an exchange between Christ and Peter. Toward the end of His earthly ministry, Jesus asked the disciples, "Who do you say I am?" (Matthew 16:15). Without hesitation, Peter responded, "You are the Messiah, the Son of the living God" (verse 16). To this Christ replied, "You are Peter, and on this rock I will build my church" (verse 18).

The Catholic Church believes and teaches that Christ singled out Peter as the leader, or foundation, of the apostolic church. Thus, it believes that Peter became the first in a long line of leaders. But if this is the case, then why did the disciples later come to Christ asking, "Who is the greatest in the kingdom of heaven?" (Matthew 18:1, ESV). And why did a dispute arise "among them as to which of them was considered to be greatest" (Luke 22:24)? Evidently the apostles didn't think Christ had set Peter apart as the greatest among them. One posited scenario is that Peter was a spokesperson for the disciples and, in that sense, was likely perceived as first among equals.

But if this were the case, then why would Peter and John be sent out by other apostles (Acts 8:14)? And why was James the leader of the first recorded council if Peter was the pope (Acts 15:12–29)?

As the gospel spread, Paul came to dominate the rest of apostolic history and even rebuked Peter (Galatians 2:11–14). He sends greetings to various believers but never mentions Peter (Romans 16), which would be expected if Peter was the bishop of the church.

So it's clear that Scripture is silent on the idea of apostolic succession: there is no unbroken line of leaders from Peter to the end of history. Despite the absence of scriptural support, the Vatican II council plunged on, stating that "it is through Christ's Catholic Church alone, which is the all-embracing means of salvation, that the fullness of the means of salvation can be obtained."[10] This is to say, sinners are indebted to the church for salvation, not Christ. What a counterfeit!

Sacraments won't save you

In Peter's epistles, the focus is on Christ and not on the church. The new birth is a gift given to humans through the resurrection of Christ (see 1 Peter 1:3, 4) and "through the living and enduring word of God" (verse 23). Faith is "of greater worth than gold" (verse 7), for humans are not redeemed by money but by Christ's shed blood (verses 18–20). And finally, Jesus "appeared once for all at the culmination of the ages to do away with sin by the sacrifice of himself" (Hebrews 9:26). There is no need for the repeated sacrifices of Christ in the Eucharist.

Note Peter's extraordinary focus on God. All blessings come directly from Him and not through a church. Faith comes "through the righteousness of our God and Savior Jesus Christ" (2 Peter 1:1). Grace and peace come "through the knowledge of God and of Jesus our Lord. His divine power has given us everything we need for a godly life through our knowledge of him who called us by his own glory and goodness" (verses 2, 3). Participating in the divine nature comes through "his very great and precious promises" (verse 4), not through the seven sacraments of the church.

But in the papal system, the Eucharist replaces Calvary. The Vatican II documents state, "The Eucharist shows itself to be the source and the apex of the whole work of preaching the gospel."[11] "Priests fulfill their chief duty in the mystery of the Eucharistic Sacrifice. In it the work of our redemption continues to be carried out,"[12] so the church can even be called "the universal sacrament of salvation."[13] "All priests cooperate in carrying out the saving plan of God."[14] Priests "exercise the work of salvation through the Eucharistic Sacrifice."[15]

Clearly, the Mass is priest centered and not Christ centered. In fact, the priest's role is central to the papal plan of salvation. Franz Xaver Esser, a Jesuit priest, graphically describes his role: "Oh priest, how superhuman and great you are, you are like Christ who commanded the wind and the sea, and who walked on the heaving waves. . . . With his scepter the priest enters heaven and takes the Son of God from the closed circle of the angelic choir and they all are powerless, they cannot prevent it."[16]

Imagine this happening all over the world by thousands and thousands of priests. Can Christ really be pulled from heaven to a priestly altar? To be sacrificed millions of times each month as if priests, and not Christ, were in charge of the continuing ministry of Christ? It hardly seems possible; it hardly makes sense; and most important, it ignores the words of Christ Himself: "It is finished" (John 19:30). Genuine worship should ascend to the only true Christ in heaven, worshiping Him for His never-to-be-repeated sacrifice at Calvary.

In addition to this sacrament is the disturbing doctrine of purgatory—an alleged destiny that follows death and gives people further time to atone for their sins. The latest *Catechism of the Catholic Church* affirms purgatory: "After death they [believers] undergo purification, so as to achieve the holiness necessary to enter the joy of heaven."[17] This means that preparation to go to heaven must be achieved after death. But how can God befriend forgiven people and then confine them to flames? The answer is simple. He wouldn't and He doesn't. The doctrine of purgatory undoubtedly collapses on the sufficiency of Christ's full payment for sin by His death at Calvary.

Replacing Christ with Mary

In the Middle Ages, believers thought God the Father "should accord to the prayers of the Virgin Mother all the consideration which a noble knight owes to the wishes of his lady, and if her interposition on behalf of all her adorers is thought by the Son of God to go to too great lengths, His Mother refers Him to the fifth Commandment."[18]

When Luther was an Augustinian monk, he "prayed especially to the Blessed Virgin, who with her womanly heart would compassionately appease her Son."[19] Luther also testified to the false picture of Christ that Catholicism had taught him: "Christ is represented as a terrifying Judge. His exacting and serious wrath was impressed on the people to such a degree that they had to flee from Him. This view was driven so deeply into the hearts of people that I and others were terrified when we heard the name of Christ. . . . They taught us to call upon the dear mother of Christ and to urge her . . . to plead against His wrath over us and to obtain His grace."[20]

Add Mariolatry to the long list of false teachings that burden millions of believers. Surely the saints are worthy of our respect and appreciation, but there is only one Intercessor and His name is Jesus Christ. He is the only one qualified to intercede in heaven's sanctuary. No human, including Mary, is fit to assist Christ's intercession. Only Christ is "the source of eternal salvation" (Hebrews 5:9); the "one mediator between God and mankind, . . . who gave himself as a ransom for all people" (1 Timothy 2:5, 6). He alone "is able to save completely those who come to God through him, because he always lives to intercede for them" (Hebrews 7:25).

No wonder the papacy banned and burned Bibles! The Scriptures expose its opposition to Christ. The counterfeit system of salvation has demeaned Christ and replaced Him with human ideas and human traditions. And unlike the Magisterial Reformers of five hundred years ago, Protestant leaders seem oblivious to these dangers.

But what about Seventh-day Adventists? What about you and me? For many of us, this is a philosophical exercise because we have never been persecuted for our faith. But the time is soon coming when buying, selling, and worshiping will be life-and-death matters (Revelation 13:1–4, 11–17). What then?

When the papacy uses the strong arm of civil power to enforce the Sunday law by a death decree (verses 1–15), "the church may appear as about to fall, but it does not fall. It remains, while the sinners in Zion will be sifted out—the chaff separated from the precious wheat. This is a terrible ordeal, but nevertheless it must take place."[21] Yes, all of this must take place, but a saving faith in Jesus will carry you through. "When these things begin to take place, stand up and lift up your heads, because your redemption is drawing near" (Luke 21:28).

———

1. Vatican Council, *The Documents of Vatican II*, 11.

2. Ibid., 23.

3. Ibid., 27, 28.

4. Ibid., 38.

5. Ibid., 40.

6. Ibid., 79.

7. Ibid., 86.

8. Ibid.

9. Ibid., 93.

10. Ibid., 346.

11. Ibid., 542.

12. Ibid., 560.

13. Ibid., 79.

14. Ibid., 575.

15. Ibid., 442.

16. Franz Xaver Esser, *Zepter und Schlüssel in der Hand des Priesters* (Freiburg im Breisgau: Herder, 1924), 15, quoted in Gerhard Pfandl, *Daniel: The Seer of Babylon* (Hagerstown, MD: Review and Herald® Pub. Assn., 2004), 81.

17. United States Catholic Church, *Catechism of the Catholic Church*, 2nd ed. (New York: Doubleday, 2012), art. 1030; cf. arts. 1030–1032.

18. Karl von Hase, *Handbook to the Controversy With Rome* (London: Religious Tract Society, 1906), 2:111.

19. Martin Luther, *Luther's Works*, vol. 54, *Table Talk*, ed. Helmut T. Lehmann (Philadelphia, PA: Fortress, 1967), 340.

20. Martin Luther, *Luther's Works*, vol. 13, *Selected Psalms 2*, ed. Jaroslav Pelikan (St. Louis, MO: Concordia, 1956), 326.

21. Ellen G. White, *Maranatha: The Lord Is Coming* (Washington, DC: Review and Herald® Pub. Assn., 1976), 32.

CHAPTER

Armageddon
and the Second Advent

The signs and symbols of Revelation are rooted in Israel's salvation history, and a careful study of the Old Testament illuminates their meaning. Understanding a challenging subject like Armageddon is possible only within the broader context of Old Testament types and recognizing their prophetic significance.

Most of the world is not biblically literate, but nearly everyone has heard of Armageddon. Pop culture has leveraged the idea into books and blockbuster movies. Armageddon sells well, but unfortunately, there is little appreciation for the true nature of this stupendous biblical event.

Battle lines are drawn

The book of Revelation highlights the global nature of the battle of Armageddon. In Revelation 14:14–20, the word *earth* is mentioned six times (ESV). In Revelation 16:12–16, the spirits of devils go to "the kings of the whole world" with a counterfeit message (verse 14), gathering the masses to their side in the battle. On God's part, the three angels' messages go to the whole world (Revelation 14:6–11), calling people to join Christ's side in the battle. The stage is now prepared for war: the three spirits of devils are pitted against the three angels and their messages. The battle lines are drawn, and the world is poised for the end-time showdown. The Bible shows that Armageddon is much more than fodder for thrilling movies. It is a winner-take-all, zero-sum struggle between good and evil.

When John has something important to say in Revelation, he repeats the point, expanding on previous explanations to clarify his message. His first mention of war comes in Revelation 12:17. Satan furiously attacks the end-time church and seeks to destroy the saints. Revelation 13 opens the curtain a little further by explaining that nearly all the world will worship Satan and his system (verses 3, 4). Those who don't follow Satan will suffer penalties, including economic sanctions and even death (verses 13–17).

Armageddon is a battle between God's people and their enemies. We know this because the Bible is not a book about secular history; it is a book about religious history—a book that follows God's people and His relationship with them. Nations are referenced only as they negatively and positively interact with God's people.

Of course, the popular image of Armageddon is a secular battle. However, the Bible indicates there is a strong spiritual component to the conflict. Note this passage that is embedded in the Armageddon section of Revelation 16: " 'Behold, I come as a thief. Blessed is he that watcheth, and keepeth his garments, lest he walk naked, and they see his shame' " (verse 15, KJV). This same message, given to the Laodicean church (Revelation 3:18), is a repetition of God's appeal to His end-time professed followers to wear Christ's robe of righteousness. This generous gift of spiritual deliverance is clearly linked to physical deliverance from the destructive forces of Satan.

Types of Armageddon in the Old Testament

The Apocalypse is a beautiful mosaic of Old Testament allusions and references—some five hundred of them. Bible students know that without a thorough knowledge of the Old Testament, it's difficult to mine the deep truths of Revelation, including Armageddon. And the primary tool to accomplish this task is one that the Reformers made good use of: this is the principle of letting the Bible interpret itself. It's tempting to jump right to the latest political headline for enlightenment, but Scripture, particularly Revelation, requires a careful analysis of the entire biblical record.

Following this approach, a review of the Old Testament literature shows that the first mention of Megiddo is in Judges 4, 5. Israel was sold into the hands of Jabin, the king of Canaan, who had nine hundred iron chariots and oppressed Israel for twenty years (Judges 4:1–4). The Israelites didn't even have a shield or a spear among them (Judges 5:8); but Deborah the prophetess told Barak, the man God appointed to free Israel, "Go! This is the day the LORD has given Sisera into your hands. Has not the LORD gone ahead of you?" (Judges 4:14). Deborah went with Barak, and God "routed Sisera" (verse 15), leaving no surviving enemy soldiers (verse 16).

The Song of Deborah poetically describes the event: "From the heavens the stars fought, from their courses they fought against Sisera" (Judges 5:20). Of special interest is the description of the battle as taking place near "the waters of Megiddo" (verse 19).

The second reference linked to Armageddon is Elijah's encounter with the prophets of Baal (1 Kings 18:16–40). Outnumbered, Elijah faced 450 priests of Baal.[1] The Mount Carmel showdown teetered on one issue: worship. Who was the true God, and who was worthy of worship—Baal or the Lord?

In order to prove that the Lord is the only true God, Elijah proposed a challenge to the prophets of Baal. The priests would offer a sacrifice to Baal, and Elijah would offer a sacrifice to the Lord. Whichever god set the sacrifice on fire was the true God. All day the Baal worshipers frantically begged their god to accept their sacrifice. They "slashed themselves with swords and spears, . . . until their blood flowed" (verse 28). But no fire fell from heaven to consume their sacrifice. No whimper of a response came from Baal. In stark contrast was Elijah's simple entreaty that his Lord show everyone that He was God (verses

36, 37). Instantly fire fell, consuming the sacrifice and the entire altar.

The prophets of Baal were subsequently slaughtered by the Kishon River (verse 40; cf. Judges 4:7; 5:19–21), emphatically showing God's displeasure with pagan worship. The Kishon River, fed by the springs of Megiddo, flows by the north side of Mount Carmel, linking both to the root meaning of *Armageddon*; "*har-megiddo*, 'mountain of Megiddo.' "[2]

God fights for His people

The prophet Malachi picks up the story of Elijah. God told Malachi, "I will send the prophet Elijah to you before that great and dreadful day of the LORD comes" (Malachi 4:5). A partial fulfillment of this prophecy was met in the ministry of John the Baptist (Matthew 17:9–13; Mark 9:9–13; Luke 1:17), who paved the way for Christ's mission. But the complete fulfillment is still in the future, for the great and terrible day of the Lord was not His first coming to save humankind but His second coming as Judge.

Much like Elijah, the end-time saints will be true to God while the rest of the world will be occupied with false worship. God will bring deliverance to the "Elijah people": "Those who keep the commandments of God and hold to the testimony of Jesus" (Revelation 12:17, ESV). Like Elijah, they will be outnumbered, but they will be miraculously delivered and the enemy will be totally destroyed.

In addition to Barak and Deborah's defeat of Sisera and Elijah's victory on Mount Carmel, there are other stories that allude to God's power to defeat evil. One such example is an Armageddon-like battle that took place against Judah. After Israel went into Assyrian captivity, Judah remained true to God for a while, but shortly the Moabites, Ammonites, and Meunites made war against King Jehoshaphat and Judah. These nations rallied "a vast army" (2 Chronicles 20:2), and an alarmed Jehoshaphat fell to his knees in prayer and fasting. "Our God, will you not judge them? For we have no power to face this vast army that is attacking us. We do not know what to do, but our eyes are upon you" (verse 12).

Soon the king received a message from God: "Do not be afraid or discouraged because of this vast army. For the battle is not yours, but God's. . . . You will not have to fight this battle. Take up your positions; stand firm and see the deliverance the LORD will give you, Judah and Jerusalem. Do not be afraid; do not be discouraged. Go out to face them tomorrow, and the LORD will be with you" (verses 15, 17).

So the next day King Jehoshaphat set out, not with an army but with a choir. "As they began to sing and praise, the LORD set ambushes against" the enemy (verse 22). This confusing tactic worked, and in utter disarray, "they helped to destroy one another" (verse 23). "No one escaped" (verse 24).

This theme is repeated in a number of Old Testament battles where God intervened and caused the enemy to kill each other (Judges 7:19–22; 1 Samuel 14:15–20; Isaiah 19:2; Ezekiel 38:14–23; Haggai 2:22). Miraculous deliverance is a recurring theme in salvation history, and these Old Testament stories confirm a marvelous truth about God: He loves to deliver His people when they face overwhelming odds.

The Exodus

No review of God's deliverance would be complete without remembering the Exodus and the parting of the Red Sea (Exodus 14:10–31). The newly freed slaves stood petrified on the banks of the Red Sea as the world's greatest army moved in from the rear. Impassable water in front of them and an impossible enemy behind them, there was no human way of escape. "They were terrified. . . . [They said to Moses,] 'It would have been better for us to serve the Egyptians than to die in the desert!' " (verses 10, 12). It's easy to fault them for grumbling, but from their perspective there was no way out. They were done. Finished. They forgot that human extremity is God's opportunity.

"Moses answered the people, 'Do not be afraid. Stand firm and you will see the deliverance the LORD will bring you today. The Egyptians you see today you will never see again. The

LORD will fight for you; you need only to be still' " (verses 13, 14). The people of Israel forgot their God, the One who protected them in Goshen while plagues fell on the Egyptians, but Moses remembered God's miracles and trusted He would perform them again.

This total dependence on God sharply contrasts with the Egyptian army's reliance on its own prowess. Pharaoh's soldiers were ready to slay the unarmed and trapped runaways. They were proud and certain of victory, but they failed to realize they were fighting the God of the universe, not a band of unarmed slaves. God drowned every Egyptian soldier in the Red Sea and opened up a path for His people to safely cross. What deliverance! This deliverance foreshadows the rescue of spiritual Israel at the battle of Armageddon.

Preparing for destruction

Drawing on the Exodus story, the seven plagues of Revelation (Revelation 16:1–21) are strikingly similar to the ten plagues that fell on Egypt (Exodus 7:14–12:30). These end-time plagues will come in response to the global false worship of Satan and his counterfeit religious system (Revelation 13). They will fall on "the people who had the mark of the beast and worshiped its image" (Revelation 16:2), "on the throne of the beast, and its kingdom" (verse 10a), and on those who will kill God's people (verses 5, 6).

For a short period of time, ten kings "will give their power and authority to the beast. They will wage war against the Lamb" (Revelation 17:13, 14). These nations, together with the United States, will enforce the Sunday law with a death decree (Revelation 13:1–15). But they soon turn on the papacy and destroy it (Revelation 17:16).

Armageddon is the ultimate victory of the Cross

God's incredible deliverance of His people and the promise of victory hinge on the most significant event in human history— Calvary. Yes, two thousand years have passed, and we're still waiting for the Second Coming, but in a sense the Judgment

Day we long for has already taken place at the cross. Calvary was Judgment Day for Satan. His fate was sealed when he sent Jesus to His death. That is why salvation history looks forward to the Cross and looks backward to the Cross. It is the focal point of everything. The Desire of Ages stumbled to Calvary and there, bearing the sins of the world, died for all human beings (1 John 2:2). Could there be a better, more concrete revelation of God's utter compassion and concern for the human race?

Since the Cross, we live in a time filled by the victory of that event. And whether we realize it or not, humankind does not move toward an uncertain future and a vague eternal destiny. On the contrary, every person can live with joy, knowing that Jesus will triumphantly return because He prevailed at Calvary. That is the good news of the gospel. Because He died and rose again, He will return. He came to His end so that we could enjoy a new beginning.

The Cross ensures the outcome of Armageddon

There are several scenes of the Second Advent in Revelation (Revelation 6:12–17; 14:14–20; 19:11–21). They document the victory that was won at the Cross. In Revelation 14, Christ comes on a white cloud, wearing a crown as "a son of man" to deliver His people (verse 14). In Revelation 19, Christ rides a white horse as "KING OF KINGS" (verse 16), with an army on white horses ready to destroy the enemy (verses 11–21).

> Then I saw the beast and the kings of the earth and their armies gathered together to wage war against the rider on the horse and his army. But the beast was captured, and with it the false prophet who had performed the signs on its behalf. With these signs he had deluded those who had received the mark of the beast and worshiped its image. The two of them were thrown alive into the fiery lake of burning sulfur. The rest were killed with the sword coming out of the mouth of the rider on the horse (verses 19–21).

An important point to make here is that the sixth plague of Revelation 16 is not Armageddon. Rather, it is a description of the two sides readying themselves for the battle of Armageddon (verses 12–21). Some interpreters view "the kings from the East" as Japan or China (verse 12), or even Israel and Palestine in the Middle East. But careful Bible students view "East" as the direction of heaven, from whence comes the sealing angel of Revelation 7:2. A few chapters later, John describes the King of kings riding forth on a white horse (Revelation 19:1). Flanked by the armies of heaven, God finally defeats the forces of evil. This second coming of Jesus is the climactic moment of the battle of Armageddon.

During His trial, in the moments before Calvary, Jesus predicted this climax to Armageddon: "I say to all of you: From now on you will see the Son of Man sitting at the right hand of the Mighty One and coming on the clouds of heaven" (Matthew 26:64). What a glorious sight it will be to see the Father and Son vaulting through the heavens on a final rescue mission! What a blessed day that will be!

------

1. Elijah also faced four hundred prophets of Asherah on Mount Carmel at the same time as the priests of Baal, but "no mention is made of what happened to the prophets of Asherah." *Andrews Study Bible*, note on 1 Kings 18:40.

2. Francis D. Nichol, ed., *The Seventh-day Adventist Bible Commentary* (Washington, DC: Review and Herald® Pub. Assn., 1980), 7:846.

CHAPTER 13

How to Wait for the Second Coming

In previous chapters, we have thrilled at the clear lines of Bible prophecy that bring hope and assurance. We know God wins the battle of Armageddon. We know Satan is defeated. We know how the story ends. And because of this confidence, Adventists have been preaching the soon coming of Jesus since the mid-nineteenth century. But still we wait—and wait.

Like most people, you've played the waiting game. Traffic jams and long lines are maddening, but you hang in there because rush hour ends and checkout lines recede. Your patience is tested, but the ordeal is survived. All's well that ends well. But what if you waited with no end in sight? What if the one thing you wanted most never arrived? From a Christian perspective, what if you waited for Jesus to return and He never came?

The importance of faith and discipline
The thought must have crossed Paul's mind as he sat shackled in a Roman prison. If anyone had cause for dismay, it was this persecuted leader. After a lifetime of beatings and jailings, he again finds himself incarcerated. Yet in spite of his circumstances, his unwavering faith is handed on to a young leader named Timothy.

With conviction, he pens a final encouragement: "For I am already being poured out like a drink offering, and the time for my departure is near. I have fought the good fight, I have finished the race, I have kept the faith. Now there is in store for me the crown of righteousness, which the Lord, the righteous Judge, will award to me on that day—and not only to me, but also to all who have longed for his appearing" (2 Timothy 4:6–8).

Paul's resolve in the face of trial is instructive for those who wait today. No one was more passionate and enthusiastic about the Second Advent than this great apostle to the Gentiles. But how could he be so confident that his patience would be rewarded? Was he delusional, or did he truly understand how to win the waiting game?

To answer this question, fast-forward nearly two thousand years, and consider the experience of a modern prisoner of war (POW). I'm talking about Vice Admiral James Stockdale. During the Vietnam War, he was a fighter pilot who emerged from the unpopular conflict as one of the most decorated naval officers in United States' military history. Shot down in 1965, he suffered for seven years in the infamous "Hanoi Hilton" POW camp. Often in solitary confinement, he had no rights, no prospect of release, and no assurance he would ever see his family again. But he always believed the United States government would come to his rescue.

Years later, Jim Collins, a business professor at Stanford University, read Stockdale's autobiography, *In Love and War*. And in his own book *Good to Great*, Collins reflects on his feelings after reading the story. "Here I am sitting in my warm and comfortable office, looking out over the beautiful Stanford campus on a beautiful afternoon. I'm getting depressed reading this, and I know the end of the story! I know that he gets out, reunites with his family, becomes a national hero, and gets to spend the later years of his life studying philosophy on this same beautiful campus. If it feels depressing for me, how on earth did he deal with it when he was actually there and *did not know the end of the story?*"[1]

How to Wait for the Second Coming

Since Stockdale was now a senior research fellow at the Hoover Institution at Stanford, Collins arranged to have lunch with him. Together they visited as they walked across the Stanford campus. Getting right to the point, Collins asked him how he dealt with being a POW when he didn't know the future.

Stockdale replied, "I never lost faith in the end of the story. . . . I never doubted not only that I would get out, but also that I would prevail in the end and turn the experience into the defining event of my life."

Collins went silent for a while.

> We continued the slow walk toward the faculty club, Stockdale limping and arc-swinging his stiff leg that had never fully recovered from repeated torture. Finally, after about a hundred meters of silence, I asked, "Who didn't make it out?"
>
> "Oh, that's easy," he said. "The optimists."
>
> "The optimists? I don't understand," I said, now completely confused, given what he'd said a hundred meters earlier.
>
> "The optimists. Oh, they were the ones who said, 'We're going to be out by Christmas.' And Christmas would come, and Christmas would go. Then they'd say, 'We're going to be out by Easter.' And Easter would come, and Easter would go. And then Thanksgiving, and then it would be Christmas again. And they died of a broken heart."
>
> Another long pause, and more walking. The he turned to me and said, "This is a very important lesson. You must never confuse faith that you will prevail in the end—which you can never afford to lose—with the discipline to confront the most brutal facts of your current reality, whatever they might be."[2]

Do you sense the tension? Stockdale was at once a pessimist and an optimist. He embraced both perspectives equally—his brutal reality *and* his faith that he would prevail. In his wise words, I hear echoes of a beleaguered Saint Paul. Like Stockdale, Paul accepted his brutal reality but never gave up on the end of the story. Not because he trusted in an earthly government but because he had absolute faith in his Redeemer. It seems paradoxical, but it also rings true: an Adventist is one who waits for the return of Jesus, boldly dealing with today yet confident that the future is secure.

Yes, times are tough, but the best way forward is to keep learning about Jesus and sharing His love. And our faith can be fortified with a robust knowledge of what God has told us about the Second Advent. What are the facts that inform our faith? Following are six important realities that you will find helpful as you wait for Christ's second coming.

When Jesus will come

Jesus' disciples asked Him one day, "What will be the sign of your coming and of the end of the age?" (Matthew 24:3). Jesus answered this question in two ways.[3]

Fact 1: We don't know when Jesus will come. During the past century, various groups and individuals have set dates for Jesus' second coming, including 1914, 1964, 1988, and 1994. During the 1990s, some people predicted that Jesus would come on or about the year 2000. However, Jesus said, "About that day or hour no one knows, not even the angels in heaven, nor the Son, but only the Father" (verse 36).

So it's useless to set dates for the second coming of Jesus ourselves or to get excited about the dates others set. Many people get burned out when date after date passes and nothing happens, and they give up all hope in Jesus' return.

Fact 2: We can know when His coming is near. Jesus did say, however, that we can know when His coming is near, just as we know that summer is near when we see leaves sprouting on the trees (verses 32, 33). And He gave us several signs by which we can know this.

One of these signs is the global preaching of the gospel. "This gospel of the kingdom will be preached in the whole world as a testimony to all nations," He said, "and then the end will come" (verse 14).

We humans will never know when every person on Earth has had a chance to hear the good news about Jesus and His offer of eternal life to all who believe in Him. But one point is very evident—it's easier today than it has been at any other time in human history to share the good news with every human being. Think of it: television, radio, books, magazines, and newspapers—and now the Internet and the World Wide Web! Given the right circumstances, the whole world could hear the gospel overnight!

The Bible also says that shortly before Jesus returns, the world will be fascinated with spiritualism and communication with demonic spirits. For example, Jesus said that prior to His return "false messiahs and false prophets will appear and perform great signs and wonders to deceive, if possible, even the elect" (verse 24). In a similar passage in Revelation, John said that "demonic spirits that perform signs" will gather the kings of the earth for the battle of Armageddon (Revelation 16:14). And Paul said that at the time of Jesus' return, Satan will come with "all sorts of displays of power through signs and wonders" (2 Thessalonians 2:9).

It's significant that today we see a rapid buildup in New Age channeling and other forms of so-called communication with the dead. This is a sign of Jesus' soon coming, and it's also a warning that we must not accept miracle workers simply because they seem to have supernatural powers. Satan can work miracles, and he performs his miracles to deceive people.

How Jesus will come

Jesus predicted that prior to His return impostors will appear at various places on Earth, claiming to be Him. "Watch out," He said. "For many will come in my name, claiming, 'I am the Messiah,' and will deceive many." That's why He warned, "If anyone tells you, 'There he is, out in the wilderness,' do not go out; or, 'Here he is, in the inner rooms,' do not believe it" (Matthew 24:4, 5, 26).

Fortunately, no one has to be deceived. There are three ways you can recognize the real Jesus when He comes. (See facts 3–5.)

Fact 3: His coming will be a public event. For one thing, Jesus' coming will be the most public event in the history of the world. The Bible says, "Every eye will see him" (Revelation 1:7), and Jesus Himself said, "As lightning that comes from the east is visible even in the west, so will be the coming of the Son of Man" (Matthew 24:27).

Not only will Jesus' coming be visible, it will also be very, very audible. Paul said, "The Lord himself will come down from heaven, with a loud command, with the voice of the archangel and with the trumpet call of God" (1 Thessalonians 4:16). And he told the church in Corinth that "the trumpet will sound" at Jesus' second coming (1 Corinthians 15:52).

Fact 4: He will come in the clouds. Jesus also said that He will come "on the clouds of heaven" (Matthew 24:30)—a fact that is repeated several times in the New Testament. For example, in Revelation, John wrote, "Look, he is coming with the clouds" (Revelation 1:7). Later, after seeing a vision of Jesus' second coming, John said, "I looked, and there before me was a white cloud, and seated on the cloud was one like a son of man" (Revelation 14:14).

Fact 5: The dead will be raised to life. Jesus said, "A time is coming when all who are in their graves will hear his voice and come out—those who have done what is good will rise to live" (John 5:28, 29). Jesus didn't say just when this will happen, but Paul explained that it will happen at Jesus' second coming: "The Lord himself will come down from heaven, . . . and the dead in Christ will rise first" (1 Thessalonians 4:16).

So you can know that anyone claiming to be Jesus is an impostor unless he appears on clouds in the sky with the sound of a loud trumpet and raises the dead to life.

How to be ready

Finally, the important question is, How can you and I be ready for Jesus' return? And the answer is the sixth important fact we need to know about His second coming.

Fact 6: You can be ready. Even some people who think they are ready for Jesus' second coming will discover they aren't. He warned, "Not everyone who says to me, 'Lord, Lord,' will enter the kingdom of heaven" (Matthew 7:21).

So what must you and I do to be ready for Jesus to come?

First, we must recognize the wrong things we've done and make them right. If we've harmed someone, we should make amends. And while God doesn't require us to overcome all of our bad habits before He will accept us, He does want us to acknowledge them and put ourselves *on the side* of overcoming them. The Bible calls this *repentance* and *confession*. We must also accept Jesus' death on the cross for our sins and ask Him to forgive those sins.

When we have met these conditions, God does two things for us. First, He forgives us. And second, He transforms our minds and emotions so that the evil things we once loved we will now hate and the good things we once hated we will now love. Christians call this the *new birth*.

The hope of Jesus' coming

Are you getting tired of pain and suffering and sickness and death? God promises that in the new home Jesus is preparing for us "he will wipe every tear from their eyes. There will be no more death or mourning or crying or pain, for the old order of things . . . [will have] passed away" (Revelation 21:4).

When Jesus comes, those of your friends and loved ones who were believers and have since died will be raised to life. They will join with God's people who are still alive on the earth, "and so we will be with the Lord forever" (1 Thessalonians 4:17). No wonder the Bible invites us to "encourage one another with these words" (verse 18).

Yes, problems linger, but the future is secure because God's promises are sure. "In the darkest days of her long conflict with evil, the church of God has been given revelations of the eternal purpose of Jehovah. His people have been permitted to look beyond the trials of the present to the triumphs of the future, when, the warfare having been accomplished, the redeemed will enter into possession of the promised land. These visions of future glory, scenes pictured by the hand of God, should be dear to His church today, when the controversy of the ages is rapidly closing and the promised blessings are soon to be realized in all their fullness."[4]

I want to be ready to meet Jesus when He comes. Please join me in renewing your commitment to Him and accepting His offer of salvation.

---

1. Jim Collins, *Good to Great: Why Some Companies Make the Leap . . . and Others Don't* (New York: HarperCollins, 2001) 84, 85; emphasis in the original.

2. Ibid., 85.

3. The rest of this chapter, with minor editorial changes, is printed with the permission of Marvin Moore, from his article "Six Important Facts About Jesus' Second Coming," *Signs of the Times*, June 2010, http://www.signstimes.com/?p=article&a=40064025600.692.

4. Ellen G. White, *Prophets and Kings* (Nampa, ID: Pacific Press® Pub. Assn., 2005), 722.

Notes

Notes